RABBITS & HARES

RABBITS & HARES

•ANNE McBRIDE•

with illustrations by
GUY TROUGHTON

Whittet Books

Endpaper shows rabbit and hare.

First published 1988
Text © 1988 by Anne McBride
Illustrations © 1988 by Guy Troughton

Whittet Books Ltd, 18 Anley Road, London W14 0BY

Design by Richard Kelly

The quotations on pp.118 and 119 from
The Leaping Hare by George Ewart Evans
are reproduced by kind permission of Faber and Faber.

British Library Cataloguing in Publication Data

McBride, Anne
  Rabbits and hares
  1. Rabbits & hares
  I. Title   II. Series
  599.32′2

ISBN 0-905483-67-7

Phototypeset by Falcon Graphic Art Ltd
Printed and bound by Oxford University Press Printing House

Acknowledgments

If I were to list by name all those who have helped with this book this section would be boring. I would also leave myself open to abuse from those who, for reasons of space or bad memory, didn't get a mention. The list would cover many years, back to the lady who gave me my first rabbit when I was five, my teachers who left me in charge of the school rabbits in the holidays, and my family who put up with being overrun by a variety of pets; my college supervisor who despaired of me ever getting my doctorate and loyal friends who liberally supplied moral support and la bonne vie throughout my thesis and the writing of this book; those who have had to suffer me rabbiting about rabbits, who have stalwartly waded their way through reams of manuscript; to other lagomorphiles who have generously given advice and information. Annabel, the Ed., for not groaning too much, Guy for giving the reader some relief from the prosaic prose and you for buying this book. To all I gladly say, Thank you. And, most importantly, to all the rabbits, wild and domestic, who have let me share a part of their lives.

Contents

Peter Rabbit, Bugs Bunny: whose name means what?

In Britain we have three species of animal that we call rabbits and hares. You could be forgiven for thinking that all three are 'ordinary' British mammals which have been part of our landscape, language and culture since history began. But you would be mistaken. The ubiquitous rabbit is a real johnny-come-lately, having been a continuous resident of these islands for a mere 800 years. The brown hare too is quite a newcomer, having arrived with the Romans less than 2,000 years ago. So, throughout the centuries while the Egyptians were building the pyramids, the Greeks were sorting out mathematics and Christ was preaching, the people of Britain shared their country with only one of the three species – the blue hare.

This state of affairs is reflected in the history of our language. The Celts and the Anglo-Saxons had words for the hare, the latter being *hara* from which came their word for that predator of hares, the Great Snowy Owl, *harfang* or 'hare-catcher'. But there were no words in these languages for the rabbit because there were no rabbits in Britain between prehistoric times and the 12th century. The first word used for rabbit was 'coney' or 'cony', an adaptation of the Norman word *conin*. It was not until 200 years later, in the 14th century, that the word 'rabbit' came into use. Again, this was derived from the French *rabette*.

At this time the word rabbit only referred to young animals, adults were still called coneys. This distinction between adults and young was apparently very important, especially when it came to mealtimes – rather as we distinguish between lamb and mutton. It was quite common for rabbits and coneys to be served up as separate courses at the same meal and there were even special instructions on how to carve the meat, with chefs being told to 'unlace that coney'.

Since the 18th century 'rabbit' has been used for animals of all ages and the word 'coney' is now virtually obsolete, only being used in legal statutes and in heraldry. But you may well come across it in the names of villages or other places, for example Coneysthorpe in Yorkshire. Nowadays, the noun rabbit tends to refer only to the animal, but it has picked up a couple of slang usages along the way. If you had lived around 1590 it would have had another quite different meaning. At that time and down to our own

century it was a slang name for someone who played games very badly, especially tennis or cricket, something Ian Botham need never fear being called! In modern slang, the verb 'to rabbit' means to talk a lot which comes from the Cockney rhyming slang 'rabbit and pork', 'to talk'.

Another term used nowadays, especially for baby rabbits, is 'bunny'. This word was invented about 350 years ago but no-one is too sure where it came from. In the days when our great-grandparents were young, earlier this century, there was a ragtime dance called the bunny-hop, presumably because it involved hopping around the floor like a rabbit. There was also the bunny-hug which was an energetic kind of dance in which the partners closely embraced each other.

Different parts of the country have had their own words for rabbits, though these are rarely used now. My favourite is the Cheshire word 'clargyman' which was the name given to black rabbits because the clergy used to wear collars made of black rabbit fur.

Today the term 'rabbit' tends to be used for adults while babies are called 'kittens' or 'pups'. A male rabbit is called a 'buck' and a female a 'doe'. Other rabbity terms are 'warren' which now means the system of 'burrows' or tunnels where wild rabbits live, and 'nest stop' which is the short tunnel in which rabbit kittens are born. A slightly different vocabulary is used when talking about hares. Adults are still called 'bucks' and 'does', though colloquially males are called 'jacks' and hares in general share pet names with cats such as 'puss', 'mawkin' and, in

Shakespeare's day, 'bawd' (*Romeo and Juliet*, II, iv). Baby hares are called 'leverets'. Being surface dwellers, hares do not live in warrens, but they do dig themselves shallow depressions in which to rest and shelter from the wind. These are called 'forms'. It is as well to know what these terms mean as you will often come across them in books on rabbits and hares, including this one.

The great number of common names given to animals over the centuries and across different parts of the world can cause a lot of confusion. As we will see, an American rabbit is not the same animal as its British counterpart – Bugs Bunny and Peter Rabbit are really quite different beasts. Because of this confusion, biologists use special names for different types of animals. The next chapter looks at the scientific names of rabbits and hares and how these came about.

'Harey' connections

Many human conditions have names associated with real or supposed characteristics of the hare. To say that someone is 'hare-brained' or 'harish' implies that they are giddy, reckless, mad and foolish – like the Mad March Hare of Alice in Wonderland fame. As we will see, the 'March madness' of hares is actually part of their courtship ritual. It used to be thought (erroneously) that hares never slept and there is an illness named from this myth. People suffering from 'Lagopthalmia' or 'hare's-eye' have permanently contracted upper eyelids, forcing them to sleep with their eyes half open. Similarly, because hares lie extremely still in their forms, not moving even when danger passes close by, it was thought, albeit wrongly, that they had poor vision

and people with short sight were called 'hare-eyed'. Well, it's certainly a nicer term than the 'four-eyes' I was called at school. Sadly, many children are born with what is known as a 'hare-lip'. This is when the top lip is split into two, the normal state for hares but not for humans (nor rabbits whose split lip is actually joined at the top). Thankfully, with modern surgical techniques this defect is easily corrected soon after birth, leaving a barely visible scar.

9

Rabbit families

Rabbits and hares belong to a group of animals known as the order *Lagomorpha*, which means 'hare-like'. The only other member of this order is the pika, or 'rock-rabbit'. At first glance, pikas don't look anything like a rabbit or a hare. They have chunky bodies, rounded ears, short legs and no tail, while the rabbits and hares tend to be larger, have long ears and long hind legs as well as the famous cotton-wool tail. However, all three show a similar pattern of teeth. This was one reason why scientists decided that these animals should be grouped together in their own separate order.

Pika.

Many people think that rabbits and hares belong to the order *Rodentia* – the rodents – which includes the mice and rats. However, the rodents have only 4 incisors, or front chisel teeth, whereas the lagomorphs have 6. The extra pair of incisors are small and located directly behind the larger pair in the top jaw. These little teeth are rounded and lack a cutting edge, and hence are only of moderate use to their owner. You can only see them if you open the animal's mouth and look behind the large upper incisors (but beware of getting your fingers bitten).

The order *Lagomorpha* is divided into two major families. It is here that we will say goodbye to the pikas who have a family status all of their own. The rabbits and hares belong to the same family, called the *Leporidae*. This family is further subdivided into 10 major genera (genera is the plural of genus), of which we in Britain are concerned with only 2. These are *Oryctolagus* (the true rabbit) and *Lepus* (the hares). Each genus is subdivided into species, which is the level of division most of us mean when we distinguish one type of animal from another, as in a lion from a tiger.

Within the 10 major genera of *Leporidae* are over 40 species of rabbit and hare. The genus *Oryctolagus* is comprised of only one species, the one with which we in Britain are familiar. This species also has a wide distribution across Europe and is well known to many of our continental neighbours. In contrast, the rabbits of America belong to quite a separate genus, *Sylvilagus* (the cottontails). What our American cousins call a rabbit doesn't look much like what we think of as a rabbit. The Bugs Bunny bunch are much more hare-like in appearance with rangy legs and long ears. Other species are strikingly different again. Take, for example, the rare volcano rabbit, sole member of the genus *Romerolagus*. This species has a very restricted range centred on the high tablelands near Mexico City. Not only is its range small, but so is its physique, with its petite ears and compact, rounded body.

One of the American Sylvilagus *rabbits, in this instance a brush rabbit.*

Different species of rabbit and hare can be found throughout the world. They occur naturally in most countries, exceptions including Madagascar, Australia and New Zealand. Mind you, the latter two countries are well stocked with the descendants of British bunny immigrants. However, of the 40-odd lagomorph species only 3 exist in Britain, and 2 of these are recent imports! These British residents are the 'European rabbit', the 'brown hare' and the 'blue hare'.

Oryctolagus cuniculus is the scientific name for the European, or true, rabbit. It is a fairly new name, having only been agreed upon by scientists in 1874. *Oryctolagus* comes from the Greek and means 'hare-like digger'. *Cuniculus* is the Latin word for an underground passage or mine, a very good description of the rabbits' notorious excavating habit.

Lepus timidus is the name the famous Swedish scientist Linnaeus gave to the blue hare back in 1758. *Timidus* means timid and the hare has, somewhat wrongly, often been associated with shyness or faint-heartedness — such people sometimes being labelled 'hare-hearted'. It is known commonly as the blue or varying hare because of its annual change of colour, from a russet coat in summer to a pale bluish white in winter — though the ear tips remain dark throughout the year.

The brown hare currently has two different Latin names, *Lepus europaeus* and *Lepus capensis*. The first of these was given to the species by Pallas in 1778 and refers to the part of the world in which it is found, namely Europe. Slightly earlier, in 1758, Linnaeus had named the hares of the African continent *capensis* — again this name refers to the animals' geographical location — the Cape of Good Hope. This distinction was happily accepted by everyone until the early 1960s when it was suggested that these two species were not in fact different but were one and the same. Consequently, it was suggested that the brown hare of Europe should be known by the slightly older name of its African counterpart, *Lepus capensis*. There is still some argument as to whether this should be so and many people, including myself, prefer to use the name *Lepus europaeus*.

Though these scientific names are very useful and avoid any confusion (or should do), they really are a bit long-winded. So to clarify it once and for all, in this book I shall use the common names of blue hare, brown hare and rabbit when talking about *Lepus timidus*, *Lepus europaeus* and *Oryctolagus cuniculus*, respectively.

Family trees.
Why use Latin?

All animals and plants have scientific names which uniquely distinguish them from other types of animals or plants, rather like our own surname and forenames. Latin and Greek are used both to describe particular features or habits of the organism and to ensure that people from different countries can be certain they are talking about the same creature.

The classification and naming of organisms is done by scientists called taxonomists. They use specific characteristics to decide where in the

Order	*Lagomorpha*			
Family	*Ochotonidae* (pikas)	*Leporidae* (rabbits and hares)		
Genus	*Ochontona* (pikas)	*Lepus* (hares)	*Oryctolagus* (rabbits)	*Sylvilagus* (cottontails) + 7 other genera
Species	*princeps* *collaris* (Rocky Mt) (collared) + 5 other species	*articus* *cuniculus* (Arctic) (European) *timidus* (blue) *europaeus* (brown) *capensis* (cape) + 20 other species		*aquaticus* (swamp) *floridanus* (eastern) · + 10 other species

A subsection of the genera and species in the Lagomorpha. *The classification system resembles an upside-down tree with branches getting smaller until single twigs represent species. There are over 40 species of* Lagomorpha.

scheme of things any particular individual should be placed. When classifying mammals, these include differences in skeleton, skull and dentition (tooth pattern). These parts of an animal tend to remain longest after the animal is dead, and fossilized bones and teeth are used to identify species, and to help piece together their evolutionary origins.

Recently, new techniques have given rise to a new method of classification – using the pattern of DNA contained in an animal's genes. (In brief, DNA is the key organic chemical, common to all living things, within which our genetic inheritance is encoded). These patterns can show previously unknown relationships between different types of animals. Though in its infancy, this modern tool may lead to some shuffling of the present groupings of animals. We shall just have to wait and see, but whatever happens, it is unlikely that the overall layout of the classification scheme into different layers will change. For our purpose we are only concerned with 4 of these layers, the order, family, genus and species. These 4 layers are illustrated for the case of rabbits and hares in the diagram on the previous page.

It is the genus and species names that scientists use most. By convention, the generic name comes before the species name and is capitalized. This is like writing my name as 'McBride anne' instead of 'Anne McBride'. Just like in a telephone directory, this system allows for easy reference – imagine having to look up all the 'annes' to see which one was 'McBride'!

LEPUS EUROPAEUS

IT WAS LEFT BY A HALF-RATE, CHEATING PHOTOGRAPHER .... SHAME HE USED THE WRONG SPECIES!!

Viva Hispania!

The wild rabbit, so familiar a sight in the British countryside, is not a native of this country and to find its origins we have, like holiday-makers, to go south to the sunny Iberian peninsula, what is now Spain and Portugal. When the ancient Phoenicians discovered Spain (around 1100 BC), they were so astounded by the number of rabbits that they called this new country *i-shepham-im*, which actually means 'the land of the hyrax'. The Phoenicians had never seen rabbits before, so the word they used refers to an animal from their own country which they felt the rabbit resembled. When *i-shepham-im* is translated into Latin it becomes *Hispania*, of which the English form is 'Spain'. So how did the rabbit get from sunny Spain to soggy Britain?

Rock hyrax.

Little is known of the rabbit from prehistoric times. A few remains have been found which could date from the last Ice Age, but the rabbits' persistent burrowing often makes it difficult to tell whether these bones are really that old or just the remains of a more modern rabbit which happened to die after burrowing into ancient deposits. It is thought that rabbits moved slowly northwards. They made their way through Spain and France, finally crossing over the land bridge that, until 5,000 years ago, connected Britain to Europe. But it seems to have been a brief sojourn. After the last Ice Age, the weather became warm and humid and, within 1,500 years, Britain was covered in vast tracts of dense woodland: a rather unsuitable habitat for rabbits. It seems that the rabbit did not survive in Britain during this post-glacial period. Certainly, the people who first left records of their language in Britain, the Celts and Old English (about 2,500 years ago), had no word for the rabbit, implying that they did not know of its existence.

A similar story seems to be true of the brown hare, of which there are no definite records until the time of the Roman invasion in the 1st century AD. In contrast, the blue hare has left fossil remains which are substantially older than the time of the last Ice Age. Being an Arctic species, it is quite likely that the blue hare has existed continuously, at least in Northern Britain, since well before the last big freeze and was the only lagomorph in Britain until the arrival of the Romans.

The Romans were very partial to hare for dinner, served in a variety of ways. Wild-caught hares were kept alive in walled gardens called *leporaria* until needed for the table. It is unlikely that hares bred in these gardens, because, unlike rabbits, they are notoriously bad at breeding in captivity. Given that the blue hare lives in mountainous country, it seems quite probable that the Romans brought stocks of brown hares with them to be released into the countryside and so provide a supply of animals for the *leporaria* and table. With the development of agriculture providing the open arable habitat it prefers, the brown hare would then have spread rapidly across the country.

The Romans also ate rabbit, but did not keep them in *leporaria*, at least not to begin with. In fact, the citizens of Rome did not know of the rabbit's existence until about 100 AD when it was finally brought to mainland Italy as a gastronomic novelty. When the Roman invaders left Britain in about 300 AD the fashion of eating rabbit had yet to spread to this outpost of the empire. The rabbit was not to be seen here until over 700 years after the Romans had left.

It has been thought that the rabbit arrived with the Normans soon after the conquest in 1066. Surprisingly, however, there is no mention of the rabbit in the Domesday Book, written in 1086. In fact, there is no written record of the species until 1176, when it is mentioned in a report about the Scilly Isles. On the basis of such evidence, or rather the lack of it, recent authorities suggest that the rabbit was brought back to Britain by the Crusaders in the late 12th century.

It is quite possible that these imports were from domesticated stock as the domestication of the rabbit had begun on the Continent in the medieval monasteries some 500 years earlier. The Pope of the time had decreed that, although Catholics were not to eat meat during Lent, fish and some animals considered to be fish were allowed. These included beaver, a fact which contributed to its extinction in Europe, hare (*Romeo and Juliet*, II, iv) and unborn or newly born rabbits. These people had an odd, or convenient, idea of natural history and the classification of animals. One outcome of the papal decree was the rapid spread of the rabbit across Europe from one monastery to another. In the process the rabbit became domesticated and the spread of these animals across the Continent was much faster than the colonization by wild rabbits, which was hampered by the dense forest areas still covering much of Europe at the time. In fact, domestic rabbits reached parts of Germany 300 years before their wild counterparts.

The monks were responsible for the domestication of the rabbit. To begin with, wild, pregnant does would be caught and brought into the monastery courtyard where, being deprived of their warren, they would drop their litter in any odd corner. It was uneconomical to kill the doe for the unborn young when the removal of the young soon after birth provided the required food and allowed the female to be remated. This then gave the monks a supply of the required delicacy at the low cost of maintaining a small permanent breeding stock within the monastery grounds. The domestication process may have begun in earnest as early as the 6th century, when it is thought the French monks began breeding experiments by selecting animals for tameness and size. Colour variations, as we see them today in domestic rabbits, were a more recent development. An early piece of evidence documenting a pure white variant is a painting done by Titian in about 1530 of the Virgin Mary and a rabbit. It's called 'The Madonna with the Rabbit', what else?

Though the rabbits brought to Britain by the 12th-century Crusaders may have come from such domestic stock, they could equally have been from captive wild populations. The Romans' *leporaria*, used for keeping hares, were later adapted for rabbits, a practice continued long after the fall of the Roman empire. These walled-in rabbit gardens were the playground of many a noble lady. Here they could indulge in the thrill of the hunt without exposing themselves to the physical demands and dangers of other sports such as boar hunting. The rabbits in these gardens were not domesticated nor bred for tameness, and so made an exciting quarry to be chased and killed before they disappeared down their burrows. The hunt was conducted, using bows and arrows, clubs and lap dogs, by ladies in long flowing dresses and wimples. But there was a major drawback to this sport: the cost of keeping the garden walls rabbitproof so that the quarry did not escape was high. One alternative was to use small islands as rabbit gardens. Queen Elizabeth I greatly enjoyed hunting and had several islands specially reserved for this purpose. To help in the hunt she had a pack of miniature beagles (23cm/9 inches high) called 'pocket' or 'rabbit' beagles. They were bred to hunt rabbits and hares and were carried to the hunt on horseback. These dogs were still popular in the late 19th century.

Rabbits were not only kept for the pleasure of fashionable ladies, they also provided a valuable source of income. By then, the meat was highly prized and featured on many a gourmet menu; in fact, no important feast was complete without it. At one Christmas feast held by Henry III in the mid 1200s no fewer than 500 hares and 200 rabbits were eaten, as well as a great variety of other meats including boar, beef and swan. But this excess was outdone 200 years later at the installation of George Neville as Chancellor of England where the menu included, amongst such exotica as porpoise and wild bull, no fewer than 4,000 rabbits. An additional economic reason for keeping rabbits was their fur. By the early 1300s England was conducting a profitable export trade in rabbit pelts and, until quite recently, rabbit fur was in demand for use in the manufacture of felt for top hats.

Before the advent of the modern commercial rabbit farms, where rabbits are kept in cages in large buildings, commercial rabbits were kept in walled-in areas. These were similar to the *leporaria* but were known as 'warrens'. The warren could be very extensive, 1,500 hectares (3,700 acres) or more. They were enclosed by banks of earth or stone walls, sometimes as much as 12 kilometres (8 miles) long, with deep foundations to prevent escape by burrowing. These walls were capped with wooden palings or gorse and, in the 19th century, with wire netting. The warren was kept in good condition and rabbitproof by an appointed warrener. It was his job to maintain the walls, control predators and disease and, of course, to catch poachers. The warrener also had to make rabbity homes for his charges. He planted prickly shrubs such as gorse and bramble to provide food and shelter and built mounds of earth, called pillow mounds, for the rabbits to burrow in. In order that he could conduct his duties efficiently the warrener lived in a special house, part of which was tall enough to allow him a good view of the whole warren.

Until the Ground Game Act of 1880 it was illegal for any tenant farmer to kill a rabbit for, in law, the rabbits were the sole property of the landowner, irrespective of how much damage was being done to the farmer's crops. Penalties for poaching were very severe, in some cases warranting the death penalty, which indicates the worth of the rabbit to the·landowner. The rabbit continued to hold a high position in terms of the whole country's economic wealth until the 18th century. Then, with the agricultural revolution, came better prices for corn and wool and the land was gradually turned over to arable and sheep farming and many warrens were destroyed. However, alongside the improvements in agriculture came an increase in feral rabbit numbers. (Feral animals are those who were once domesticated and looked after by man but which have reverted to the wild state.) These were being encouraged by the gentry for their sporting value, and indirectly rabbits were also helped by the stringent control of predators, the aim of which was to preserve game birds, such as pheasant. All these changes in the social and farming spheres led to such a dramatic increase in the feral rabbit population that by the late 19th century they were causing substantial crop damage. It was realized that something had to be done to protect the interests of both the farmer and society. Hence the Act of Parliament in 1880 which allowed ordinary people to kill rabbits. It is interesting to note that the same social issues of the 18th and 19th centuries, concerning the prestige of the rabbit as a sporting animal, led to the massive problem of rabbit infestation for which Australia also became famous (see below).

The effect of the rabbit on the British landscape, and its cost to the country in crop damage, resulted in the 1939 Prevention of Damage by Rabbits Act. This gave local authorities the power to force landowners and occupiers to destroy rabbits. In 1947 this power passed to the Ministry of Agriculture. In spite of these steps, crop damage remained high and farmers continued to suffer. Rabbit densities reached as high as 50 adults per hectare (124 per acre) on the mainland and even 100 per hectare (248 per acre) on some islands. Between 1950 and 1953, 40 million rabbits were killed annually in Britain and still the problem would not go away.

The methods used for rabbit control were not as grandiose as steps taken in Australia, which included the erecting of many thousands of miles of rabbit fencing. Gassing, shooting, warren destruction and ferreting were all conducted on a grand scale in both countries – but in vain. In 1953, it seemed the final solution had been discovered: myxomatosis.

Myxomatosis is a contagious disease specific to rabbits; that is, other animals, except occasionally hares, do not catch the disease. It is considered in depth later in this book, but for now its importance lies in its effect on the British rabbit population. In one word, this effect was devastating. Myxomatosis was introduced by man to Britain in September 1953 and, by 1955, had spread throughout the country. Over 99% of the wild population died, with the rabbit population reaching its lowest level in 1956 at which it stayed for the rest of the decade. In 1954 it was made illegal to deliberately spread the disease and rabbit clearance areas were established in an attempt to maintain rabbit numbers at this new low. But during the 1960s the population began to recover and special clearance societies were formed to try and prevent further increase on farmland. In the 1970s, the strengthening of the population was becoming more obvious, especially in the south-east, as rabbits were becoming more resistant to the virus and the myxomatosis virus lost its potency. Now, in the 1980s, it is estimated that the rabbit population is approximately 20% of the 1953 pre-myxomatosis level and still increasing.

The spread of the rabbit through Australia and the dramatic recovery from its own version of the Black Death shows that this apparently defenceless, oh so sweet and harmless creature is biologically very adaptive and quite a match for the ingenuity of man.

Rabbits down under

The Australian rabbit problem began with the arrival of the first fleet in 1788. Then, and for the next 50 years, many domestic rabbits were imported. By the 1850s rabbits were kept in most towns and cities, primarily for food. Some escaped or were liberated, providing an alternative to kangaroo hunting. In the main these feral populations were small and remained contained, giving little cause for concern. One possible reason they stayed small was due to predation; any variations from the normal wild colour (see p.32) would not be well camouflaged and would easily be picked off by birds of prey and other predators.

There is only one authenticated report of wild rabbits being imported to Australia. In 1859 Mr Thomas Austen imported 24 rabbits to his estate in Victoria, Australia. He specifically asked that the cargo be made up of wild-caught British rabbits – perhaps he felt these would make the best sport – though it seems that at least some of the shipment were in fact agouti, that is, wild-coloured, domestic animals. The rabbits were released onto his land and their progress was monitored. By 1865, only 6 years

after the original release, over 20,000 rabbits had been killed on Austen's estate alone. By 1866 the rabbits had spread to Queensland, some 800 km (497 miles) away, having crossed and colonized New South Wales at the amazing rate of over 100 km (62 miles) per year. This feat is all the more remarkable when you remember that these colonizations could not have occurred in a single rabbit generation, the migrating rabbits must have stopped to breed and rear their young. In part this highly successful spread was due to the lack of competition from other grazing mammals. The rabbit, with its faster and more efficient breeding rate, was able to compete very successfully against native marsupials which are the indigenous grazers. But, just as in Britain, the sheer density of rabbits had a severe impact on the local flora and farming. The Australian rabbit soon gained significant economic importance – as a pest.

By 1900 the situation had become desperate and the Australian authorities tried to cope in various ways, all of which were ineffectual and some extremely costly. The effort put into finding a solution is best exemplified by the barrier fences. Thousand upon thousand of kilometres of rabbit fencing were erected in the hope of protecting those areas of the country which were still rabbit-free. One fence, known as No.1 Fence, in Western Australia was 1,760 km (1,100 miles) long, and took 5 years to build, being completed in 1907. Part of it ran through virtually unknown country along the edge of the Great Sandy Desert. Bore holes had to be sunk every 20 km (12½ miles) to provide water for the thousands of men and draught animals employed. The fencing materials had to be carried by pack animals, including camels, on average 300 km (186 miles) from the nearest railway, and sometimes more than 600 km (373 miles). But the fences didn't work, partly because in some places they were built too late but mostly because they couldn't be maintained.

In hindsight, it's easy to say the barrier fences were bound not to work, but times were desperate and, for the Australians, they seemed to offer hope. As well as the fences, there were specialized teams of rabbit exterminators who, in the 1940s, had a new weapon – the burrow ripper. This machine, powered by a tractor, ripped out rabbit warrens up to a depth of 0.75m. Thousands of them were used in the 1940s and 1950s in the rabbit war. Then myxomatosis was introduced as the final weapon, but, as in Britain, it was not as successful as hoped and the war continues.

Where are they now?

Most of us who wander, or drive, particularly in the evening or early morning will have seen a wild rabbit. The most numerous and widespread of our lagomorphs, it is common throughout mainland and offshore Britain up to an altitude of about 600m (2,000 ft).

There are two major features that make an area a desirable rabbit residence. First, the presence of short grassland feeding areas is important. Young rabbits can easily die of exposure by getting wet in long, damp grass but, by persistent grazing, rabbits create and maintain preferred short turf conditions (lawns are excellent – as are golf courses). The second feature is the quantity and quality of available cover. Rabbits make a succulent meal for many a British carnivore and rely on a quick dash to the safety of the burrow, or other cover, to escape. As they only move short distances to conduct their daily business, such cover has to be close to the feeding grounds. It can be composed of scrub, undergrowth, boulders or even the spaces in drystone walls. So it is unlikely that you will find rabbits in areas of rank, long vegetation or dense close woodland. Instead, look for them where areas of short grass are frequently interrupted by clumps of secure cover. In hedgerows and railway embankments, on downland and duneland, in waste tips and suburban gardens (including Mr McGregor's lettuce patch) the rabbit is quite at home.

The brown hare is most numerous in the agricultural lowlands of mainland Britain, particularly the eastern counties such as Norfolk, but can be seen throughout the country up to altitudes of 500m (1,640 ft). It is absent from parts of north-west Scotland and it is not found in Ireland apart from a few, small, isolated introduced populations. Introductions of hares have succeeded on some larger islands such as Wight, Anglesey, Mull, Arran and Skye but, in general, unlike with rabbits, island introductions have not survived.

The brown hare is originally a species from the open steppes (vast plains devoid of forest) where it relies on its ability to run long and fast, rather than on boltholes, to escape its enemies. Consequently, because cover is not essential, though desirable, hares can do well on arable farms and pastureland, provided the density of livestock is not too great. However, while hares are common in most arable areas, modern intensive farming methods do not always maintain suitable habitats for them. The main problem with these methods is that they tend to create a food shortage

Distribution of the British lagomorphs.

■ present

▦ possibly present/probable

□ absent

RABBIT

BROWN HARE

MOUNTAIN HARE

25

between harvest time and the emergence of winter crops. But hares are likely to be present on those farms where large areas of crops are divided by shelter belts or contain long grass strips which supplement the lean periods of crop unavailability. As with rabbits, the best time to spot hares is in the evening. During the day, they remain hidden in their forms. These are scraped out so that the resting hare is at ground level, and therefore very inconspicuous. A little bank of scraped earth at the back protects the hare from the prevailing wind and acts as a springboard for the escape run should it be disturbed.

Oddly enough, brown hares often congregate and live on airfields, even Heathrow. They seem to delight in racing alongside airplanes as they land or take off. It's not known what the reason is but it has been suggested that the hares are 'playing' with the planes – pitting themselves against another fast moving object, rather like dolphins who swim alongside ships. Hares also seem to like noise and vibration, often drumming enthusiastically with their back feet for no apparent purpose. The British poet Cowper, who kept pet hares in the 18th century, noted that they seemed to enjoy the noise of thunderstorms, which are not dissimilar to the roar of jet engines. Another obvious attraction is the abundant lush food supply found on the grass stretches between runways. Still, it's a long way from the peace of a Norfolk field.

While the brown hare may be an old acquaintance of the jet-setters, few of us will have had the privilege of seeing a blue hare. Indigenous to

(Opposite) *Blue hares on snow-covered heather moor: male chasing female in early spring.*

Ireland and the highlands of Scotland, it is most frequently seen on the grouse moors of Scotland. Here the management of the heather for grouse provides an extremely suitable habitat for blue hares. Like the grouse, its favourite food is heather. Introduced populations of blue hare also live in the Peak District (above 300m/984ft), near Bangor in Wales and on some northern islands such as Shetland and the Outer Hebrides. In Ireland, blue hares live at lower elevations than on mainland Britain. This may be because there is no substantial competition from their brown cousins. The few introductions of brown hare to Ireland are recent (19th century), small and scattered. While they may have resulted in localized displacement of the blue hare, they have not as yet had any significant effect. Any such major takeover would in any case be a gradual process. Nowadays on the mainland the blue hare is restricted to the uplands, but this may not have always been the case. Prior to the arrival of the brown hare, the blue may have lived in more lowland country. Where it would have been partly dependent on the nature of the woodland. Areas with brambly undergrowth would not have been suitable, but open woodlands could easily have been inhabited by blue hares as they often are in regions of Scandinavia.

The blue hare feeds mostly on heather and upland pasture and rarely on crops, but then crops are not often grown at such heights anyway. Frequenting dry, rocky hilltops as daytime shelters, it rests beneath old heather. The blue hare is also best seen in the evening when it comes to the, usually lower, feeding grounds.

Clues

Areas occupied by rabbits are often characterized by distinct types of vegetation. Rabbits don't like to eat nettles, ragwort or hemlock and these are often to be found growing on the disturbed soil near a warren. Warrens are usually dug on slopes, which provide better drainage, and the burrow entrances are easily spotted as round holes 10–20 cm (4–8 inches) wide. Nearby may be communal latrines, often containing hundreds of tightly packed, round faecal pellets. Sprinklings of pellets are also found in small horseshoe-shaped scrapes of bare earth. Rabbit runs or pathways are another distinctive feature around warrens. Rabbits are rather unadventurous travellers and use familiar paths. These can be easily traced through the undergrowth. In fact, so conservative are rabbits and hares that they usually put their feet in the same place each time they use a run, leaving a series of bare patches along the route. Often tell-tale bits of fur can be spotted on bushes and barbed wire. Areas of close-cropped grass are usually a good indication that rabbits live nearby, as are grazed crops at the edges of fields. In winter rabbit tracks are obvious in snow, distinguishable from those of hares by being smaller.

Hares also leave conspicuous paths. Blue hares tend to run up and down hills, rather than along the contours. Hares maintain pathways by frequently pruning the heather tips. Both species of hare make forms. Those of the brown hare are shallow depressions in long grass, scrub or ploughed land, while the blue hare's tend to be deeper, often in long, old heather whose stems have been bitten off to a height of a few millimetres.

Wait and see

As with any wildlife watching, if you wish to watch rabbits and hares, you need a good deal of patience, stealth and luck. The first thing, of course, is to find a suitable area and to look for clues to inform you that the species is actually in residence. Having established this crucial piece of information, the next move is to reconnoitre the area for cover from which you can view your quarry. This may be anything from shrubs to the bough of a tree. To watch hares you will probably need a pair of binoculars as usually there is little in the way of cover available to enable you to get very close.

Once you have selected your site and made sure it is inhabited, then pick your evening, preferably a dry one — rabbits don't like coming out in the rain any more than we do. Establish yourself in your cover, making sure you are downwind of the rabbits, well before sunset. Then, keeping as quiet as you can, wait and watch. If you are very lucky you may be able to see for yourself many aspects of rabbit life which are described in this book. I have been lucky enough on occasion to watch newly emerged kittens tentatively investigating the space around their burrow entrance, slowly gaining confidence and emerging farther, apparently celebrating their new-found freedom with bouts of leaping and kicking of their young limbs.

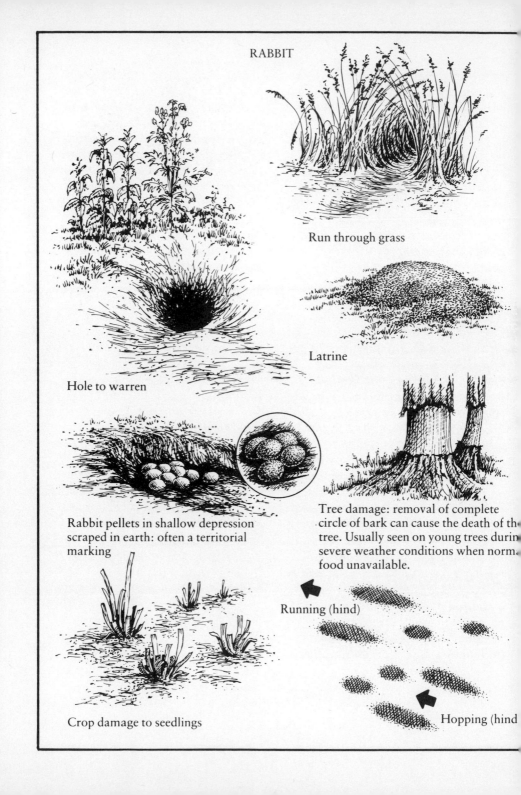

RABBIT

Run through grass

Latrine

Hole to warren

Rabbit pellets in shallow depression scraped in earth: often a territorial marking

Tree damage: removal of complete circle of bark can cause the death of the tree. Usually seen on young trees during severe weather conditions when normal food unavailable.

Running (hind)

Crop damage to seedlings

Hopping (hind)

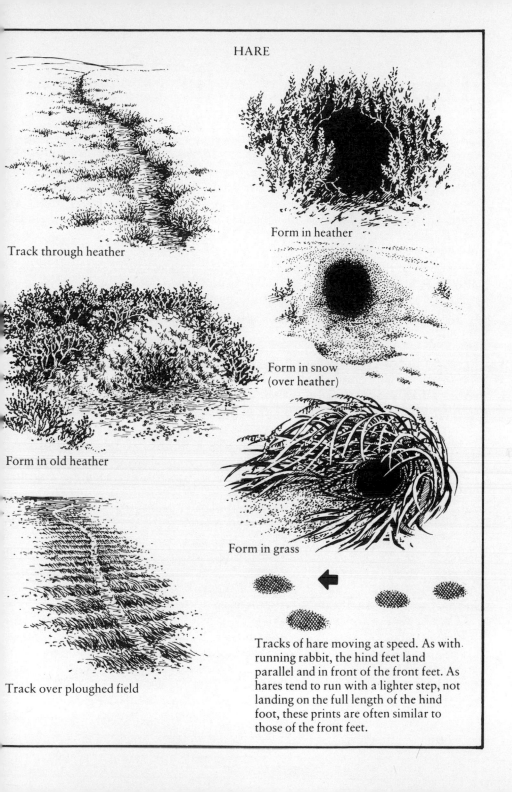

HARE

Track through heather

Form in heather

Form in snow
(over heather)

Form in old heather

Form in grass

Track over ploughed field

Tracks of hare moving at speed. As with
running rabbit, the hind feet land
parallel and in front of the front feet. As
hares tend to run with a lighter step, not
landing on the full length of the hind
foot, these prints are often similar to
those of the front feet.

Top hats and tails

The British lagomorphs, with their strikingly long hind legs, short fluffy tails and big ears, cannot be mistaken for any other British mammal (except a bunny-girl). It is relatively easy, however, for the uninformed to confuse rabbits and hares. Rabbits are smaller than hares with shorter ears and hind legs. A rough comparison is that the ears of a rabbit are about a third of the length of the head, whereas those of a brown hare are about half the head length. The long ears of both the brown and blue hares have distinctive black tips and their hind legs are proportionately much longer than those of the rabbit, so much so that, when moving, the rear end of the animal is lifted higher than the rest of the body.

Rabbits and hares are covered in a short dense coat of fur. It is similar in composition to that of squirrels, with the undercoat overlaid with curly fine hairs and longer guard hairs. The guard hairs are banded and have tips which contain less pigment than the stem of the hair and thus look lighter. The pattern of the medulla cells, seen through a microscope, is one where the cells are arranged in longitudinal columns which, in the shield region, interweave and branch before rejoining one another. This pattern is quite different from that of other orders, but it is not at all easy to distinguish between the hair of rabbits and the hair of hares.

Rabbit fur is usually of an agouti (grey-brown) colour over most of the body with a more orangey patch on the nape of the neck and greyish white on the underparts, including the underside of the tail. Variations in colour from this basic wild pattern are uncommon, though in some areas black rabbits may make up a fifth of the population. Albinos, piebalds (black and white) and skewbalds (brown and white) are rare. They tend to be found only in island populations where there is a lower risk of predation than on the mainland and so such badly camouflaged animals have a greater chance of survival. The rabbit moults once a year, starting with its head. The thicker winter coat does not involve a change of colour. The moult starts in March and is complete by October.

The brown hare moults twice a year. The first moult starts in mid-February and lasts until midsummer. Starting along the back, progressing down the limbs and ending at the head, the brown hare grows its summer coat of a warm brown colour with white underside, black ear tips and black upper surface to the tail. The autumn moult starts early in the season and begins with the head, in reverse order to the spring moult. The resulting winter coat is thicker and redder in colour though the white belly and black ear tips and tail top remain.

The blue hare is the champion moulter, not merely once like the rabbit, nor twice like the brown hare but three times a year. The first moult is

Differences between brown hare (above) and rabbit (below), showing proportionately larger size of hare and longer ears and hind legs.

Sept-Feb (white)

Feb – May (whiteish brown)

June – Sept (brownish white)

The three faces of the blue hare.

from February to May (white to brown), the second from June to September (brown to brown) and the last from October to February (brown to white). It is a smaller, more compact animal than its brown cousin with much shorter ears, also black tipped, and a tail which is white both top and bottom. The summer and autumn coats are dusky brown and grey-blue underneath. In winter the coat is white all over, except the ear tips, which stay black. In fact this is not quite true, for in many cases there is not a complete change from autumn to winter coat and it has been found that the extent of the moult is in part determined by the temperature of the environment; the colder the weather the more complete the moult.

Whilst hares show colour change across the seasons, both they and rabbits show no difference in colour between the sexes, and at a distance it is not always easy to distinguish males from females. The more experienced eye can distinguish between the blunter, rounder head of the male and the longer, finer features of the female.

At the height of the breeding season, the male's testes are descended and at their largest (in rabbits about 3.0 × 0.8 cm) but, as they are tucked tight under the animal, they are not visible from a distance. In the non-breeding season the testes are withdrawn into the body. Close

Male rabbit (above) with broader head than female (below).

RABBIT

female   male

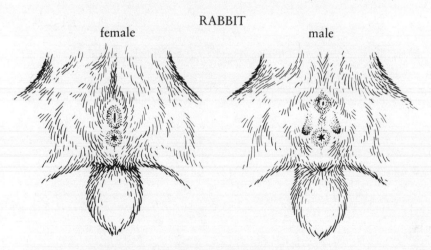

Female rabbit (left) and male rabbit (right).

examination will show that the female has a slit-like genital opening under the tail whereas the male has a round one. With experience you can accurately sex animals only a day or two old by examining them.

The last, but not least, external feature of rabbits and hares is their feet. The neat rounded forepaws seem incongruous when matched with the long shoe-like hind feet. All three species have 5 toes on the front feet and 4 on the back, but tracks rarely show this. Why? Well, because the sole of the foot is completely covered by an insulating coat of hair – another feature unique to the *Lagomorpha*. This covering has gripping qualities which means the animals can easily cross smooth, slippery surfaces such as rocks and snow. The fur also acts as a shock absorber. This quality, combined with constant regrowth of the fur padding, means the animals can move over hard surfaces comfortably with no damage to their feet from wear and tear. In fact, on hard surfaces, this is superior to hooves which quickly become damaged, unless like domestic horses they are shod, and to the padded feet of animals such as dogs which are easily cut and rubbed raw. However, on soft ground, such as marshland, the rabbit-type foot is at a disadvantage as the fur quickly becomes matted. Some experts think that, because only lagomorphs have furry soles to their feet, it is evidence that, back in the mists of evolutionary time, the ancestral lagomorph lived on hard ground such as rock, hard plains or snow.

Hind foot of hare.

Be alert

The position of rabbits and hares in the food chain means that early warning systems are the name of the game. To this end they have developed very sophisticated detection systems, the most obvious being their ears, but additionally their noses and eyes. The ears seem to be ludicrously large for their neat heads. This large surface area means that the ear can 'catch' more sound waves than a smaller one. This is enhanced by the ability to move one ear separately from the other, thus being able to listen in two directions at once.

Scents as well as sounds are carried on the breeze and can be very useful in detecting foes before they get too close to do any damage. The action of the forever winking nostrils of rabbits and hares is made all the more obvious by their split lip. The moistness of this exposed surface of the top lip enhances the animal's ability to detect scents, as does the wet nose of a dog and the 'Flehmen' behaviour seen in animals such as horses and deer. The Flehmen response is when the animal curls the top lip back towards the nose and breathes in when detecting (tasting) an interesting odour.

The eyes are placed well to the side and top of the narrow head and, especially in hares, seem to be quite bulging. This location and prominence of the eye gives the animal a wide field of vision — it can see virtually all the way around and above its head. This means it can spot any friend or foe approaching from any direction.

Vital Statistics

	RABBIT	BROWN HARE	BLUE HARE
Overall colour	*Mar–Oct* grey-brown on top grey-white belly orange-brown neck	*Feb–Aug* brown on top white belly	*Feb–May* whiteish brown on top grey belly
	Oct–Mar as above	*Aug–Feb* as above but redder	*June–Sept* brownish white top grey-blue belly
			Sept–Feb white all over
Top side of tail	Black/brown	Black	White
Ear tips	Brown	Black	Black
Length of ears from notch	60–70 mm	90–105 mm	60–80 mm
Length of hind feet	75–95 mm	130-155 mm	125–170 mm
Average adult weight			
Male	1·5kg (3·3lb)	3·5kg (7·7lb)	2·7kg (6lb)
Female	1·5kg (3·3lb)	3·7kg (8lb)	2·9kg (6·4lb)

Inside the beast

Now you know the clues, it's easy to tell which is a rabbit or hare from the outside. But what about from the inside? Here too there are differences which set them apart from other mammals and from each other.

The most obvious feature of the lagomorph skeleton is the difference in the length of the front and back legs. The long hind limbs of rabbits and hares are efficient and powerful propelling machines, to the point that when the animal is moving fast the forelimbs are virtually redundant. They merely give a smoothness to the movement which is lacking in a purely hopping animal such as a kangaroo. The forelimbs are used when walking or trotting but are fairly primitive and are not particularly specialized even for digging, which is a major rabbit activity.

The driving force behind the swiftness of the lagomorphs is the set of large muscles attached to the hind limbs. In order that they can work to peak performance, these muscles must have a good supply of oxygen and

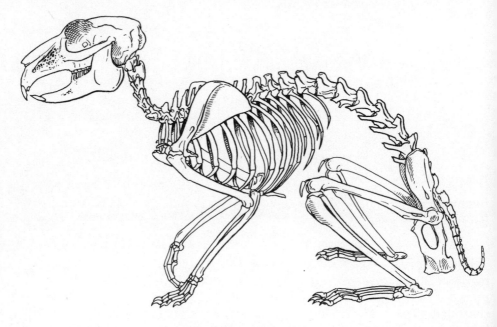

Rabbit skeleton.

energy. These are provided by the heart and blood system. It is here that the rabbits and hares differ. The rabbit's heart weighs about 0·3% of the total body weight whereas for a hare this figure is 1–1·8% Even in the fast-moving, energetic squirrel the heart is only 0·6% of the total weight. The volume of blood contained in the veins and arteries is also relatively greater in the hare than in the rabbit. This means that a proportionately larger amount of energy and oxygen can be carried around the body, pushed along quickly to where it is needed by the strong pumping of the large heart. So while the long limbs and large muscles give both the rabbit and hare great speed, it is the proportionately larger heart and blood supply that gives the hare its exceptional powers of endurance for which it is famed and which enable it to out-distance its pursuers.

As every runner knows, energy for muscles originally comes from a healthy diet and efficient digestive system. The food processing department of the lagomorphs is unique in the animal kingdom. Rabbits and hares are true herbivores, that is, they are wholly vegetarian, and, thanks to their specialized digestive system, they can survive on a relatively low quality diet.

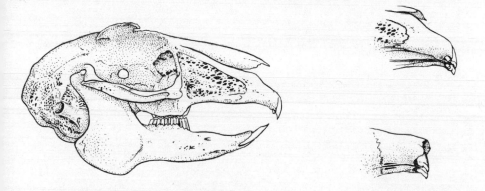

Brown hare skull (left); (above right) top incisors of lagomorph and (below right) top incisors of rodent, in this case squirrel, showing one of the distinguishing features of these two orders, namely the lagomorph's extra pair of incisors.

Food processing begins in the mouth and, we have already seen, the lagomorphs have an extra pair of incisors hidden behind the larger cutting pair. While the extra pair have little functional value, the same cannot be said of the cheek teeth, the molars and pre-molars. These are specialized for chopping and grinding grass and other vegetative matter and are

Misaligned teeth, showing excessive abnormal growth.

adapted to enable the animal to chew both forwards and sideways, ensuring that the food is finely ground before being swallowed. The teeth grow continuously, as do our fingernails. They therefore must be continually worn down by eating hard foods such as bark and carrots and, more importantly, by the grinding action of the teeth. If for some reason the teeth aren't worn down, for example if the rabbit has lost a tooth or the top and bottom jaws are misaligned, then the teeth will become pathologically long. This may prevent the animals from eating at all, or cause nasty injury by slowing growing back into the head.

In order to obtain the maximum amount of goodness from their diet, different groups of animals have developed a variety of digestive techniques. Many herbivores, such as sheep and cows, chew the cud, that is, they regurgitate partially digested food, chew it again and reswallow it, finally passing it in the normal fashion. The lagomorphs too pass most (about 80%) of their food twice through the digestive system, but in a different way.

In animals that chew the cud the food does not pass right through the system until it has been swallowed for the second time. In contrast, the lagomorph's food actually passes right through the intestinal system twice. During the day, when wild rabbits are resting, and in the middle of the night when they tend not to be grazing, a special type of faecal dropping is produced. Like ordinary rabbit droppings, these are round and dark, but instead of being hard and dry, they are soft, moist and covered in a slimy mucus. They never actually hit the ground, for in a very swift action the animals bends down and takes them straight from the anus and swallows them, without chewing them.

In simplified terms, food passes from the stomach to the upper intestine and then into the appendix and caecum. In the lagomorphs the main digestive process, that is, the release of nutrients from the food, occurs at the end of this journey in the bacteria-filled appendix and caecum. The

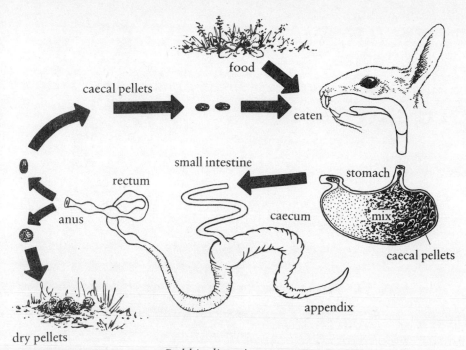

food

caecal pellets

eaten

small intestine

rectum

stomach

anus

caecum

mix

caecal pellets

appendix

dry pellets

Rabbit digestive system.

bacteria do the hard work of breaking down the cellulose walls of the plant cells and so release the nutrition for absorption by the rabbit gut. But absorption of these nutrients into the body mostly occurs earlier, in the upper intestine. So, in order to get the full nutritional value out of its food, the lagomorph must pass it through the system twice, firstly to break the food down and release the nutrients and then again to absorb that goodness into the bloodstream. The droppings that finally pass onto the ground are made from the indigestible parts of the food. This method of digestion is known as 'refection', and may have other advantages. For instance, it allows rabbits to stay below ground, with their own internally carried food supply, for up to a few days at a time when the weather is bad. In addition, this 'take-away' system means that rabbits and hares need only be out grazing in the open, where they are in constant danger, for as long as it takes to eat enough grass to fill their stomachs once a day. Unlike constant grazers such as horses who eat and digest continuously, refection means that the main part of the digestive process can take place in the safety of the burrow or form.

Foes afoot: natural predators

Rabbit in alert posture and (right) in scrub habitat.

The rabbit has many natural enemies and suffers a high level of mortality. In Spain, rabbits are eaten by over 20 different species of predator, and make up over a fifth of their diets. In Britain, dogs and foxes catch rabbits by stalking them and using the element of surprise to snatch them in the open. Cats also catch baby rabbits in this way, but healthy adults often tend to be more than a match for the average cat. Rabbit kittens are dug out of the nest stop by hungry foxes and badgers. But public enemies numbers one and two in the rabbit's view must be the stoat and weasel (and polecat in Wales). These animals are thought to hunt in family groups (mother and juveniles) with some members going down the rabbit burrows, flushing out the residents which are then caught by the rest of the pack waiting at the exits. Buzzards and harriers will attack rabbits, although only larger birds, such as golden eagles, are strong enough to carry off the adults. Owls and hawks tend to hunt kittens and sick adults, thus keeping the rabbit population healthy (or dead). Rabbits that have been killed by disease, road accidents or predators make a welcome meal for all kinds of animals including rooks, crows, magpies, foxes, rats, hedgehogs and beetles.

GUY TROUGHTON

With so many enemies it is not surprising that rabbits have developed several tactics for eluding capture. When surprised, the rabbit will bolt for the nearest hole, often twisting and turning in such a way as to make it impossible for the predator to keep up. However, if it should be caught, a healthy adult will try to defend itself using its slashing teeth and giving powerful kicks with its hind feet – the original rabbit punch. These hind feet are equipped with sharp claws which can inflict a nasty injury.

As in everything, prevention is better than cure, and rabbits are very vigilant animals, with highly developed senses of hearing, vision and smell. Being in this constant state of alertness when away from the comparative safety of the burrow helps to ensure that the rabbit has warning of the approach of any predator. The feeding behaviour of rabbits epitomizes this alertness. A feeding rabbit will frequently interrupt its grazing, lifting its head to survey the area, often sitting upright on its back legs in order to get a better view. Studies of the behaviour of wild populations have shown that the frequency with which an individual interrupts its feeding alters depending on how many other rabbits are around. The more rabbits, the less time an individual needs to spend looking and the more time it can spend feeding. This is because the rabbit can partly rely on the vigilance of the others to warn it of any danger. The more rabbits there are, the greater the number of eyes, ears and noses acting to detect any enemy. If danger is detected the rabbit concerned thumps the ground with its hind feet to warn others nearby. The sound also reverberates underground, warning those below not to surface. The white underside of the tail, or scut, is clearly visible in a fleeing rabbit and this too acts as a signal for others to retreat to the safety of the nearest burrow. These warning signals enable an individual rabbit to eat in a more relaxed manner than would be possible if alone.

A recent study has shown that feeding rabbits may have to be more or less alert depending on where they are. It seems that if rabbits are feeding in a field alongside which runs the hedgerow cover in which they have their burrows, then they change their defence strategy according to where in the field they happen to be. If close to the hedgerow then they are very vigilant, in case some sneaky predator like a cat creeps through the undergrowth to spring a guerilla-type attack. Similarly, if in the open field over some 35m (115 feet) away from the burrow, they again must be extra alert. This distance represents a fairly lengthy sprint for a rabbit. Should a fast-moving predator such as a dog or fox appear, then the rabbit must ensure it has adequate warning so it can dash back to the burrow before being caught. If feeding somewhere between these two areas, the rabbit can afford to relax slightly as it is likely to have sufficient time to escape either a sneaky or a fast attacker.

The burrows themselves act as barriers against many larger predators. The tunnels are narrow, only 15cm (6 inches) in diameter, occasionally widening to about 40cm (16 inches). These wider points act as passing places for the underground rabbit traffic. While some animals, such as badgers, can dig rabbits out of their burrows, they are less likely to do so if the soil is heavy. Heavy soils also allow the rabbits to dig deeper tunnels without fear of the roof collapsing. The deeper the tunnels, the longer it takes a predator to dig them out and thus the greater chance for the rabbit to escape. Warrens are not built to any pattern and a large warren will have been randomly added to by generations of rabbits – maybe over several hundred years. The result is a maze of twisting, interconnected, narrow tunnels which serve to confuse any predators small enough to enter.

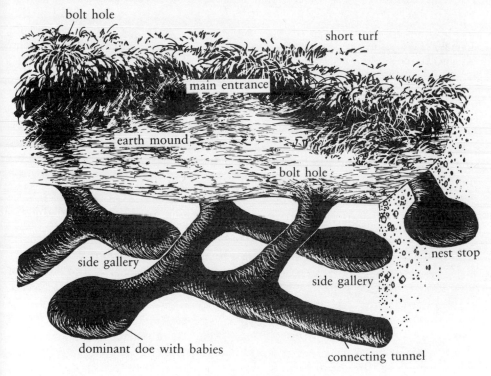

Section through rabbit warren.

Should a rabbit be pursued into the warren by a predator, such as a stoat, there are many escape exits available. In a warren covering 100sq m (1,000 sq ft) there may be over 50 holes. The main entrances to the warren are constructed from the outside, leaving tell-tale mounds of earth, but rabbits also dig a number of holes from the inside. These secret doors are often hidden in bushes and, because they are dug from the inside, there is no external sign of excavation. These holes often drop vertically into the ground for half a metre or more. This means that the rabbit must jump straight up out of the hole, a feat not so easy for a pursuing stoat.

The reason why rabbits live in social groups may be related to the high level of predation they suffer. On the surface, the more rabbits there are keeping an eye out for danger then the more likely any single rabbit will have enough warning to escape. Underground, it is easier to dig and maintain a tunnel system with several rabbits than it is with one or two. Also, there may not be very many suitable areas for digging in the locality, forcing rabbits to live in larger groups. If the soil is not strong enough to support an extensive tunnel system, as in sand dunes, rabbits tend to live in smaller groups than those found in stronger soils such as chalk downlands.

Unlike the adults, kittens in the nest stop are defenceless and rely on their mother for protection. She protects them in two ways. Firstly, she draws as little attention as possible to the nest by visiting it very infrequently, usually only about once a day. Secondly, when she leaves the nest she carefully blocks up the entrance with earth, stamping it down with her back legs. This makes the nest stop less obvious and also reduces the chance of any predator smelling or hearing the kittens, which are sealed off underground. Should a predator find the nest and dig out the entrance, then the kittens will all jump about and squeak energetically, maybe in an attempt to scare the intruder. Unfortunately, this is not very effective and a nest that is discovered is unlikely to have survivors.

When the kittens are older and have emerged to the surface, their mother will try to protect them from all comers. More often than not she will be unable to save her offspring; sadly on average less than 10% of rabbits born ever grow up to become adults. If this were not the case the rabbits would quickly incur a massive population explosion.

It is estimated that young hares suffer a similar level of mortality during their first year. The fox is their major predator, although owls and other birds of prey and feral cats would not dismiss a meal of an unwary leveret. Unlike their rabbit cousins, hares do not have burrows to run to and must rely purely on their fleetness of foot to escape their enemies. An adult brown hare can clock up speeds of 72kmh (45mph). In comparison the best recorded speed for a greyhound, over a short distance, is just under 67kmh (42mph) and for a mounted racehorse just over 69kmh (43mph).

Hare in its form.

When chased, hares will often follow familiar pathways, along which they can travel at full speed with little fear of bumping into unknown obstacles, and so outpace their pursuer. As is common knowledge to the hunting fraternity, the beleaguered hare will often change direction, or 'jink', in an attempt to confuse and outwit the hunter and his dogs. During the day, hares will rest in shallow forms which they have dug. These shelter them from the wind and provide concealment. Indeed you may almost step on a hare in such a form before it moves, for the combination of the shallow depression, its own colouring and complete stillness is a very good camouflage strategy. If not disturbed, these forms are often re-used and the hare goes to great lengths to ensure that their location remains hidden. When leaving or returning to the form, it will often double back along its track, or make a sudden 90-degree turn from its original course followed by a long leap, of 4m (13 feet) or more, perhaps landing in marshy ground where its scent will not lie. These sneaky tactics break up the continuity of scent, leaving a difficult trail for any would-be predator to follow. If disturbed when in the form, the hare does not simply get up and run. Instead, it will use the raised back of the form as a springboard, starting its escape with a dramatic bound of several metres.

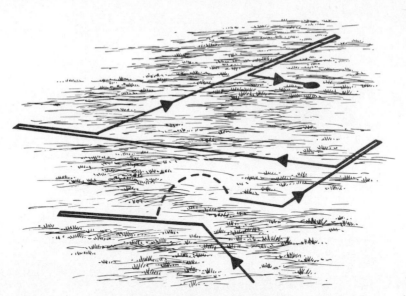

(Above) Evasive tactics of brown hare returning to its form. (Right) Brown hares by the Devil's Den, Wiltshire.

In addition to all their natural predators, rabbits and hares are harried by man both in and out of the sporting field. Sadly, their natural escape mechanisms are frequently of no help. Often they are the victims of fast cars which can and do outrun a fleeing rabbit or hare, or of modern, efficient agricultural harvesters which can easily trap and give a bloody death to a leveret. The hare is an important game animal, pursued by packs of beagles and harriers to cries of 'see-ho!', while the rabbit acts as target practice for many a sporting gun. The poor rabbit's unfortunate distinction of being a pest means it is further persecuted by both farmer and gardener, being trapped, gassed, shot and poisoned. Not that the hare is safe from the latter as many agricultural herbicides and pesticides can prove fatal. Indirectly, the use of herbicides also affects these animals by reducing the diversity of plant species available, thus cutting the food supply across the seasons. Populations can be drastically reduced by disease, such as coccidiosis and, in the rabbit, myxomatosis. Finally severe weather conditions also increase mortality by lowering the animal's resistance to disease and, more directly, by causing flooding of nests and drowning of kittens, or hypothermia in juveniles. So all in all, life as a lagomorph is not as pleasant as it may appear for, as Pliny so aptly wrote, it 'is born to be all creatures' prey'.

Myxomatosis

Frequently, man puts nature to his own use. One such instance is the case of myxomatosis. In 1953 this disease was deliberately, though not officially, introduced to Britain specifically to wipe out the rabbit pest. Nineteenth-century improvements in agriculture created habitats favourable to rabbits and predators, themselves under attack from gamekeepers, were unable to prevent the inevitable population explosion.

Myxomatosis is a disease caused by the introduction of the myxoma virus into the rabbit's body. It occurs naturally in some *Sylvilagus* species resident in Central and South America. Because of the long association between virus and host in these species, tolerance has been built up and these animals merely suffer a temporary lump at the infection site. However, myxomatosis, which is specific to rabbits and rarely affects hares, has a quite different result for the non-resistant European rabbit.

The virus is carried on the mouthparts of blood-sucking insects and so is passed indirectly from one rabbit to another. In Britain the main carrier is the rabbit flea. Within a week of being infected the victim's eyes begin to ooze a watery discharge. A couple of days later swellings, filled with pus, appear on the eyelids, nose, base of the ears and ano-genital region incapacitating the rabbit who no longer can see or hear. The rabbit usually

(Above) *Myxomatosis infested rabbit with swollen eyes and ears, causing blindness and deafness.*

dies within 11–15 days of first catching the disease.

When first introduced to Britain, the virus caused the death of 99·99% of rabbits who were exposed to the disease. Now, though a permanent feature of the British rabbit ecology, the relationship between the virus and the rabbit has been, and is, slowly changing. So far, these changes can be divided into three distinct stages.

In the first stage, as said, only some 0·01% of animals who contracted the disease survived. Once having survived the disease, the rabbit becomes immune for life and cannot catch myxomatosis again. It seems that these survivors, when breeding females, were able to pass on some immunity to their offspring, probably via the placenta. This acquired immunity was short-lived but it did mean that young rabbits, under about 2 months old, who became exposed to the myxoma virus had a greater chance of surviving and becoming immune.

The second stage concerned a change in the virus itself, into a range of viruses of different strengths. The less virulent strains were more successful because they had a longer period of time in which to be transmitted to a new host rabbit before their original host died. By the 1960s moderately weaker strains of the myxoma virus were prevalent; these caused only 70–95% mortality. This meant that a greater number of rabbits exposed to the disease survived and were able to pass on their acquired immunity to their offspring.

The final stage was that of the appearance of genetic resistance as opposed to immunity. In the mid-1970s baby wild rabbits were kept isolated for 2 months. By this time any immunity they had acquired from their mother would have worn off. These rabbits were then injected with the myxoma virus but only some of them died. It seemed that the third stage in the relationship between rabbits and myxomatosis had been reached, that is the rabbits had developed a genetic resistance to the disease. In other words they had acquired an inherent ability to survive an infection of the disease, at whatever age they became ill, even though, when infected, they showed all the usual external symptoms.

As the level of resistance increased there was a compensating increase in the virulence, or strength, of the virus. This was because these more potent strains no longer suffered the disadvantage of killing their hosts, and because the weaker strains were less effective in infecting the now more resistant host, they gave way to stronger, more potent strains. This spiralling trend of increased resistance on the part of the rabbit causing increased virulence on the part of the virus, so causing even more resistance in the rabbit, seems to be continuing. It is speculated that eventually genetic resistance in the host will have developed to the point where the virus will have no more effect on British rabbits than it does on its original *Sylvilagus* hosts.

At present, resistance levels are such that the mortality rate of infected rabbits is 40–60%. Some of these no doubt would have survived the illness if they had not been killed by predators, cars or shooting during the incapacitating stages of the disease. This level of mortality means that myxomatosis, while not proving the agriculturalists' final solution, still contributes significantly to the management of wild rabbit populations.

Can hares and rabbits co-exist?

As myxomatosis rarely affects hares, it gave scientists an opportunity to try to answer a long-posed question. Were rabbits and brown hares mutually exclusive? That is, was it true that these two could not live in the same area? Hare numbers not only increased after myxomatosis, but there was also colonization of new areas. Many of these had been used previously by rabbits, such as areas of woodland. Hares even started using rabbit burrows for breeding. At first glance this may seem to be evidence that these species were in fact mutually exclusive. But, of course, the reason for the increase in hares is not as simple as that. Agricultural changes, notably mechanization, in the late 1950s and 1960s led to an increase in field size and a preference for arable crops rather than grass production (combine harvesters don't need to eat grass). Such areas and estates which, pre-myxomatosis, had been

completely arable, did not show any post-myxomatosis boom in hare numbers. So, if competition with rabbits does not fully account for the increase in the hare population, what other factors were involved?

Firstly, the overall increase in the height of ground cover after myxomatosis meant that there was much better cover available for leverets. This combined with the general change in the diet of predators to smaller prey items further ensured better survival rates. In addition, the hare is an important game animal and general policies of game preservation reduced predator pressure on the hare. Similarly, the cessation of rabbit trapping helped the hares who were often mistakenly taken in the traps. Finally, the reduction in rabbit-spread diseases, which also affect hares, such as coccidiosis, and stomach worms also supported an increase in hare numbers.

Plague and pestilence

The disease most people associate with rabbits is myxomatosis. It certainly is the most serious with which they must contend, but is by no means the only one to which they can fall victim.

Next to myxomatosis, the major threat to the rabbit population is from a disease called coccidiosis. There are eight species of the coccidiosis parasite, single-celled organisms which live in the rabbit's gut. Only one of the eight causes the rabbit any major illness. This particular species is called *Eimeria stiedae* and is problematic because, unlike its cousins, it is not content to remain in the rabbit's gut. Instead, it enters the bile duct and works its way into the liver. Its occupation of this, one of the rabbit's vital organs, can cause the death of its host. However, as we have seen with myxomatosis, if the rabbit survives this attack of coccidiosis, it then becomes immune and can never again be infected by *E. stiedae*. As a consequence, coccidiosis is more usually seen in young animals.

A rabbit whose general health is under par, because for example it is fighting a coccidiosis infection, is more susceptible to other diseases. One such is called yersiniosis. This is caused by a bacterium known as *Pasturella pseudotuberculosis*, which gets into the rabbit through contaminated food and water supplies. Once inside, it produces lesions in the gut and passes throughout the body affecting organs such as the liver, spleen and lungs. It is a chronic disease and has nasty symptoms such as diarrhoea, emaciation and finally death. Yersiniosis is also fairly common amongst hares.

Another bacterial disease which has occasionally been reported in both rabbits and hares is plague. This is more commonly associated with rats and it may be that the lagomorphs get the disease by the transfer of fleas from infected rats. This could happen in situations where rabbits and rats share the same burrow complex.

Rabbits also share their lives with a number of other creatures. Inside the rabbit live several species of worm, while the outside is often infested with a variety of fleas, ticks and lice.

Rabbits can be infected by any, or all, of the three roundworm, nematode, species. These have divided the rabbit's gut neatly amongst themselves. The first species, *Graphidium strigosum*, lives in the stomach; the second, *Trichostrongyius retortaeformis*, lives in the small intestine, while the last, *Passalurus ambiguus*, makes its home in the caecum.

The other major internal parasite group are the tapeworms, or cestodes. Rabbits can be infected by 4 species of tapeworm, 3 of which belong to the same genus, *Cittotaenia*. The fourth belongs to the genus *Andrya* and its species name is *cuniculi* (recognize it?). Tapeworm infestation is common and up to 50% of adult rabbits will act as host for some pretty large specimens, up to 400mm long and 10mm wide. Another species of tapeworm, *Taenia pisiformis*, spends only part of its life cycle in the rabbit. In the early part of its life it resides in the liver of the rabbit. Here it does little damage and merely waits until the rabbit is killed and eaten. Then the worm can be passed on to its main host species, namely foxes and cats.

Rabbits also have several external parasites who like to get rich on rabbit pickings. In general, these are more of an annoyance rather than a danger, unless infestation is severe. In such cases, as for example an acute loading of bloodsucking lice, the loss of blood and resulting anaemia could be very important. Another problem is the possible injury to sense organs which can be caused by the inconsideration of creatures like warble flies. These flies lay their eggs on the head of the rabbit. Sometimes the developing larvae can cause severe damage to the rabbit's eye, which doesn't exactly increase the rabbit's chances of survival.

Perhaps the best known ectoparasite is the rabbit flea, *Spilopsyllus cuniculi*. This creature made its claim to fame by being the primary agent in the transmission of the myxoma virus in Britain. The rabbit flea makes its living by sucking the blood from its host. In a manner reminiscent of a

Rabbit flea.

Hammer horror film, the flea's own life cycle is completely dependent on the rabbit population. For, unless it has fed on the blood of a pregnant doe and of newborn rabbits, the flea is unable to reproduce. After the doe has given birth, her consignment of fleas leave her body to land on the kittens. Here they gorge themselves on the sweet, young blood and then reproduce. The new generation grows up inside the rabbit's nest and then find hosts of their own.

These then are some of the smaller creatures associated with rabbits and which may or may not cause illness and death. While few have common names, the Latin ones are fun tongue-twisters and have an appropriate meaning. I'm sure you noticed that several rabbit parasites share a specific name with their host.

Rabbit habits

Rabbits are gregarious creatures whose social organization revolves around the warren. A colony of several dozen rabbits may inhabit a large warren. The colony will be divided up into distinct social groups each of which may contain from 2 (usually a male and female) to 8 adults. In the larger groups there are usually more females than males, and group members tend to be closely related through the female line. Kittens born into the group are tolerated until they reach sexual maturity at about 4 months. As the breeding season progresses, the warren becomes more and more crowded with kittens. The adults become steadily more aggressive towards the older kittens and drive some, mostly males, away. In general, young females remain in their original social group. It is this that results in the close blood ties of the group. In contrast, young males disperse to join new groups or even to join strange warrens where they tend to be fairly readily accepted while young. A few rabbits, mostly male, do not live in any social group. Known as 'satellite' males, they tend to be either very old animals who have been driven out by younger ones or to be males in their first year who have yet to find a home. These satellite males roam widely and usually live on the surface, resting in shallow holes, or scrapes beneath bushes and hedges.

Each member of a group has a particular social position, forming a social order called a 'dominance hierarchy', with the dominant animals having authority over those below them, the subordinates. A position of dominance gives an animal priority access to food, shelter and, in the case of males, to breeding females. Dominant females gain preferential access to the best breeding sites. Amongst the males the hierarchy is quite rigid and often linear with male A being dominant or over male B which is dominant over male C. Dominant males tend to be older and heavier than their subordinates. In contrast the females are generally more tolerant of each other. There may be a single dominant doe, but those females below her co-exist peacefully enough. The exception to this is during the breeding season, when females have been known to bite and rip a rival to death in competition for a particular breeding site.

Each rabbit group defends a specific area known as its territory. The size of the territory depends on the size of the group, the number of rabbits in the area and the food supply. It can vary from as little as a quarter of a hectare (0·6 acre) to as much as 6 hectares (15 acres). The rabbits are not

Dominant buck in late afternoon sunshine: not a care in the world!

confined to this area alone, for they also frequent a larger, undefended space, known as their home range. The home ranges of different groups can sometimes overlap, perhaps at more distant feeding sites.

Between August and January, rabbits are not involved with the activities of courtship and motherhood. The group seems to relax, territories are not so rigorously defended and the strict dominance hierarchy is weakened. It is at this time that migrant young of the year become integrated into new groups.

At the start of the new breeding season, in late January, there is a resorting of each individual's place in the group as the social hierarchy is restructured and territories once again are marked out. It is now that new groups and burrow systems may be formed. If the warren is overcrowded, there is likely to be a limitation in the number of suitable digging sites. Females may need to disperse in order to select a new suitable site, which they will vigorously defend against other females. The females' digging and aggressive activities soon attracts the attentions of males. These males proceed to sort out their own relationships to each other. Thus, a new stable group, which may consist only of a single breeding pair, and its new burrow system, is formed. Mind you, as far as the latter is concerned, the male's contribution is usually only a few perfunctory efforts at digging.

It is the job of the males of the group, and especially the dominant male, to defend the territory. He does this in two ways. Firstly by marking the boundaries with his scent so that any intruder recognizes that he has crossed a frontier and, secondly, by attacking and driving off any intruder bold enough to stay and argue the point.

Rabbits have very sensitive noses and an acute sense of smell. Smell is one of the major forms of communication between individuals. Rabbits of

Male rabbit scent marking with chin gland.

both sexes produce special odours, pheromones, in their urine and from glands on their chins and under their tails. We know that these pheromones inform rabbits about an individual's sex, reproductive state and position in the hierarchy. They probably contain a lot of other information about which we have no knowledge. The dominant male makes good use of these pheromones to mark out his territory, so much so that to another rabbit the area must seem to be drowned in this smell.

He rubs his chin on the ground so much that the fur becomes matted with dirt and encrusted with the gland secretions. He chin marks any prominent object such as fence posts, tree trunks and bushes. Not only inanimate objects get covered in his scent, but he will also mark other rabbits in his group – demonstrating to them just how dominant he is. This marking of others is often chin marking but sometimes involves spraying the hapless subordinate with urine. The anal glands under the tail are larger in the dominant male and impart a scent to his faecal droppings. As well as randomly depositing droppings around the area, the male and other group members leave large quantities of faeces at specific, prominent sites called latrines. All these signals help to inform strange animals about the owners of the territory. They also help to boost the confidence of resident animals as is demonstrated by the activity of the subordinate males. While the dominant male patrols and scent marks the whole of the territory, his subordinates confine their activities to small portions of it. Using the same techniques of scent marking, these males stake out their own little patches. Within this restricted area they can sometimes compete successfully against the dominant male for access to females.

In addition to marking out their own territories, dominant males are not averse to a little trespass. Naturally, when on such expeditions they try to avoid the resident rabbits, but should they happen to meet, then the trespasser will behave as if he were a subordinate. He may either merely avoid the occupant by making back for his own territory, or adopt a submissive posture. This involves lying down close to the ground with ears pressed back flat against the head. Meanwhile, the resident will continue to approach, restlessly nibbling the grass, stopping to rub his chin, scent mark on the plants or frantically dig at the ground. If the trespasser ignores these displays of dominance and neither retreats nor adopts the submissive pose, then a fight is likely to ensue. To some extent this too is ritualized, involving chasing, scraping of the ground and stiff-legged runs past each other. Physical violence rarely occurs, usually having been forestalled by all this ritualized aggression. But when it does occur, it consists of powerful kicks from the back legs, with rabbits often grabbing

A dominant (left) and subordinate (right) rabbit.

each other's necks as they kick and tumble about, but fights rarely result in death.

Rabbits live most of their lives in semi- or complete darkness. They spend their days in their underground burrows, emerging at dusk to feed, to court and patrol their territories. In such a world vision is not the most important sense and for the most part communication relies on scent, with sound playing a minor role. Rabbits do denote anger and pleasure by a range of soft throaty growls. Apart from these, the only other sound they make is a high-pitched scream, reminiscent of a young terrified child. This the rabbit emits when caught by a predator. It probably serves to warn others of the danger. They will rapidly return to the burrow until it is once again safe to emerge.

Hare habits

Because the hare has not had the dubious prestige of being considered a major pest, it has not been afforded the same degree of study of its habits. However, what research has been done seems to suggest that the social life of the hare is far less complicated than that of its rabbit cousin. Only further research will reveal whether this picture is accurate.

Hares are basically nocturnal: feeding, courtship and mating take place during the hours of darkness, though in the short nights of summer the activity period often starts before sunset and extends after sunrise. During the day, hares lie up in their individual forms in open fields or in nearby

Blue hare in form during blizzard.

woods. Woods are used more during the cold winter months because they afford more protection against the worst of the weather. The forms are spaced well apart and for the daytime, at least, the hares are alone.

Come dusk the hares leave their forms and travel to the feeding place, generally staying in the same area for the rest of the night. For many centuries it was thought that hares were solitary animals, but this appears not to be the case. When feeding, they seem to prefer to be in groups. They don't feed right alongside each other, but in loosely associated collections. As with rabbits, it has been shown that feeding in a group means that an individual hare need not be so vigilant – the same story that two (or more) pairs of eyes (and ears) are better than one.

As hares spend much of the active part of their time in association with others, they too have simple rules by which their social affairs are conducted. They do not seem to practise scent marking or other ritualistic territorial behaviours; nor does it seem that they have well defined territories to defend. But the males do show a loose dominance hierarchy, though not as pronounced as in rabbits. Competition for food is unusual amongst hares since food tends to come in field-size packages so there is enough for everyone. However, it is known that at sites of preferred foods dominant individuals will drive away younger or subordinate ones by adopting an imposing stiff-legged posture. The only time when enforcing one's position in the hierarchy becomes really important is during the

Brown hare: stiff-legged dominant approach.

breeding season. Females are a commodity worth fighting over and the more dominant males will defend their rights of access with great vigour.

There is one odd facet of hare behaviour, rarely reported, which also seems to be associated with the breeding season. There are reports of anything up to forty hares, male and female, sitting in a wide circle with one or two frolicking in the centre. No one seems to know why such assemblies occur, though some believe it may be an arena in which males display to females. Your guess is as good as mine.

Wine and roses

The courtship of rabbits and hares is relatively uncomplicated and to the point. During the breeding season the males are actively seeking as many females as possible that are ready to be mated.

When a buck rabbit first finds a female that interests him he spends a good deal of time loping after the lady in question, always remaining a respectful five metres or more behind her. Gradually, he approaches nearer and, assuming a stiff-legged posture, proceeds to circle or parade to and fro in front of her. In this posture, the white underside of his tail can be clearly seen, pushed up as it is by his tense haunches. It makes a dramatic contrast to the darker colouring of his back and this part of the courtship is aptly called 'tail-flagging'.

Tail-flagging male, showing off his assets to nearby female.

The female often plays hard to get and continues to feed, barely noticing her suitor. Sometimes, the male will make his case more apparent by squirting a jet of urine over his prospective mate. This is performed very speedily and on the move, the male twisting his hindquarters and urinating as he runs past the doe. The doe usually ignores this behaviour, merely shaking herself (who can blame her? It's hardly an alluring overture), or she may decide to retreat to a burrow.

However, persistence on the part of the male can be the key to success. The more interested female will often go and lie by the male with her ears laid back. This is a signal for the buck to demonstrate his affection by nuzzling her, licking her head, and sniffing her body. But this may not

necessarily lead to mating. Even at this late stage, either partner may simply lose interest and move away or the female may decide to reject the male. A female who is definitely interested and willing to mate has usually indicated this by flicking her tail in response to his tail-flagging performances.

The actual act of mating is very quick, taking only a few seconds. The male straddles the doe with his fore legs, often gripping her neck with his teeth. After a few thrusts he ejaculates, at which point he may momentarily lose consciousness and fall sideways off the female. Copulation may be repeated, the couple staying side by side and licking each other in the interim, but usually, after mating, each partner resumes his or her previous activities.

Reproduction in hares is equally polygamous. A male hare will mate with as many females as he can, dominant males usually being more successful than their lower-ranking counterparts. In the night or so prior to her heat a female is guarded by a male which remains quite near her, chasing off any potential rivals and giving them a sharp bite if he catches them. As the female approaches her 'heat', the male becomes progressively more attentive. He follows her more closely, sniffing the ground where she has been. If she grows tired of his persistent attentions she will turn in her tracks, rear up and give him a good boxing with her forepaws. This is what is commonly known as 'mad March hare' behaviour. Until quite recently, it was thought that these boxing matches were between rival males, but it is now known that it is the usually larger female fending off

Boxing hares.

the advances of a too amorous male. The behaviour occurs throughout the breeding season, which lasts from mid-February to mid-September. However, it is more noticeable in early March at the start of the breeding season. This is partly because all the females tend to come into breeding condition at about the same time and also because crops are short which makes it easier to see the hares. Competition for females is hot and it is not unusual to see one being followed by several males. As with rabbits, the actual act of copulation is perfunctory and ends with the male giving a little jump away. Having mated, the male and female go their separate ways – the male to look for yet another female.

The joys of motherhood

Perhaps the most important part of an animal's life is the rearing of its young. It's what all that eating, avoiding enemies, courtship and fighting lead up to. They are designed to keep the animal fit and able to reproduce itself. The successful rearing of the next generation not only ensures the species continues to exist, but also that some of the successful parents' characteristics, via their genes, are kept in the population to better equip future generations to survive, adapt if necessary and reproduce too.

The rabbit is one of nature's more prolific breeders, though, as we have seen, only a small proportion of bunnies born ever get to be parents. This is probably just as well, for in Britain a single female has the potential to produce thirty young each breeding season: the population could, in theory, grow to be fifteen times as large as it was the previous year. Not only would the countryside be knee-deep in rabbits, but the rabbits would soon suffer all the horrors of overpopulation, such as serious food shortages and declines in the health of individuals.

In Britain, the rabbit breeding season begins in late January and continues to the end of July, with a peak in the number of litters produced between April and May. However, in most years, a few females will be pregnant outside these months. Once fertile, at the start of the season, the female is in a state of continuous oestrus until she is mated. This means that eggs are regularly produced in the ovaries though they are not ovulated, that is, released into the Fallopian tubes, until copulation occurs. This mechanism, known as 'spontaneous ovulation', increases the likelihood of any egg which is released becoming fertilized, as it is only released when sperm are present. It takes three or four days for an egg to mature and therefore female rabbits come 'on heat' about every seven days for two to three days at a time. During this time they show an increased interest in males and a willingness to adopt the mating position.

The pregnancy lasts about thirty days and as soon as the litter is born the female again becomes fertile and starts to produce eggs. This is the post-partum (after-birth) oestrus. Within twelve hours of having had her babies a female can be pregnant again. Thus, except at the beginning and the end of the breeding season, a female is likely to be nursing one litter whilst pregnant with the next. So, during a single season a female can produce between 4 and 6 litters, each containing an average of 5 kittens.

Not all pregnancies are successful. In areas with a high population more pregnancies terminate naturally, with the loss of all embryos, than in low density populations. Similarly, in high density areas, the breeding season is curtailed. So it seems the rabbits have their own means of forestalling a population explosion. Before the advent of myxomatosis, many populations were very dense and half or more of the litters conceived were terminated. Unlike many mammals which abort their dead embryos, the rabbit reabsorbs them and the placenta, through the wall of the uterus. This unusual process is called 'resorption' and has the benefit of not wasting natural protein.

Baby rabbits about two days old.

For the female that successfully remains pregnant, preparations for motherhood must be made. During the last two weeks of her pregnancy she will start to make a nest for her young. First, she finds a suitable site, generally within the group's territory. This may be a blind end off a main burrow in the warren, or she may dig a special breeding burrow, a 'nest stop'. These nest stops are short, up to 2m (6 feet) long, single entranced tunnels, ending in an enlarged chamber. Old breeding tunnels from the previous season may be used, but it is unusual for a female to use the same site more than once a season. In Britain, most rabbits use a nest stop which is built away from the warren in some isolated spot. This is probably a precaution against the main burrow predators, stoats and weasels. While some of the hidden, isolated stops may be discovered by badgers and the like, they are not all found. In contrast, work in Australia has shown that young or subordinate females breed in isolated nest stops, whereas more mature or dominant mothers give birth in the main warren system. It may be that Australian rabbits do not have as many underground predators to worry about as do British ones, making the main warren the more attractive proposition as a place in which to raise their young.

No matter where they decide to have their young, the females must prepare a nest. This they do any time between 2 and 8 days before giving birth. The breeding chamber is filled with grass and dead plants. These she carries in her mouth, and many trips are needed. The mother-to-be hollows out the mound of plant material, using her head and forepaws, before lining it with soft fur plucked from her belly and flanks. It is into this warm, cosy and comfortable nest that the young are born.

The young are born blind and helpless. The mother licks them clean, and eats the umbilical cord and placenta. Occasionally at this stage, some mothers get a bit carried away and may inadvertently kill their offspring by eating vital bits of them, while luckier youngsters may just lose an ear tip or two. This cannibalization appears to be more common in domestic rabbits, in young, less experienced mothers or those in high density or stressed populations. However, presuming all goes well, the mother crouches over her babies to nurse them. At the end of the nursing bout, she abruptly takes her leave. As she re-emerges on to the surface, she carefully blocks the entrance to the breeding tunnel with soil, making it and its occupants less easy for a predator to detect.

The mother only returns to her babies once in 24 hours, usually at night. These visits are short, lasting only 3 minutes, just enough time for the young to be nursed. The first few nursing bouts tend to be longer, around 5 minutes, presumably because, during these early visits, the young are not as adept at suckling as they are when older. My own work on nursing rabbits has shown many instances where the kittens are nursed more frequently than the average once per 24 hours. The record was held by one mother who made seven nursing visits in a single day (almost as many as a human mother). On the other hand, some mothers were decidedly less dedicated, and occasionally skipped days, nursing their probably extremely hungry babies only once in a 48-hour period. However, the kittens didn't seem to suffer and all grew up strong and healthy.

After about 18 days, the mother begins to plug the nest stop less securely on her departure and the young begin to emerge. Soon, she must prepare for the next lot of youngsters. When the older brood are about 25 days old she ceases to return at all and, like it or not, they are weaned. The abandoned kittens usually leave the vicinity of the nest a few days later to join their mother's social group where, ever hopeful and confused, they will, for a little while, attempt to suckle any passing adult.

The type of maternal care shown by rabbits is known, for obvious reasons, as 'absentee care'. It is an unusual strategy for mammals, especially for a species whose young are born in a very undeveloped state. Indeed, the rabbit is believed to be the only mammal which has adopted this form of care. On average, a rabbit mother spends only 0·1% of her day with her young. In contrast, a mother rat will spend an average 90% of her day huddled up in the nest with her newborn babies.

Suggestions have been put forward as to why rabbits have evolved this system of minimal care. Most likely, it acts as a defence mechanism. Rabbit mothers are not very good at face-to-face confrontations with predators, preferring to take to their heels and dash for safety. So it is unlikely that they would be able to protect their babies, whereas a rat mother will bravely attack any intruder to the nest. It seems that the rabbit mother can provide better protection for her kittens by leaving them well hidden, and by visiting them infrequently so as to draw as little attention to them as possible.

Hares have adopted the same absentee strategy. Indeed, apart from a few modifications here and there, it seems to be another common feature of the *Lagomorpha*. Unlike rabbits, leverets are born fully furred, sighted and mobile. Accordingly, there is no need for the mother to build an elaborate nest to keep them warm. Instead, she gives birth to her litter of 1 to 4 babies out in the open. Just like a rabbit, she cleans them and eats the afterbirth. Hares seem to be less liable to cannibalize the young by mistake, probably because the furry leverets make more of a contrast to the afterbirth than do the almost carcase-like baby rabbits (also leverets can get out of the way should their mother get too energetic). After cleaning them, she nurses the young and then departs. Within a few hours the leverets move off a short distance from the birth site. They don't remain together, but lie, crouched down and very still, several metres apart.

Leveret about two days old.

Each day, approximately one hour after sunset, mother and young meet again to nurse at the birth place. Sometimes, leverets belonging to another litter turn up but these are not turned away, the mother merely nurses them as if they were her own. In contrast to the rabbit's crouch, the hare mother sits bolt upright to nurse. In this way she can keep a sharp lookout for danger. For the first week, nursing bouts may last up to 8 minutes, but they soon fall to about 3 minutes. During the last minute of the nursing bout, the leverets turn over on their backs and the mother licks their ano-genital area. It is thought that the babies urinate at this time and that the mother ingests the urine. This would prevent any urine smell marking the birth place, which otherwise may attract passing predators.

After nursing, the young again disperse but to a different spot from where they spent the previous 24 hours. As they get older, they rest further and further away from the birth place. When they are about 4 weeks old, the young are only nursed for a minute or so. These shorter nursings only continue for a few days after which the mother no longer returns and the young are on their own.

Hare nursing babies.

Supermums

The breeding season for hares lasts from mid-February to mid-September, during which time a female can produce 3 to 4 litters, each containing up to 4 kittens. Like the rabbit, hares produce eggs continuously in the ovaries until they are mated. They too are spontaneous ovulators, releasing their eggs only in response to copulation, thus ensuring a high fertility rate. Again like rabbits,

female hares become fertile as soon as they have given birth, and sometimes even before. In the latter event the female hare can be successfully mated and, although already pregnant, have two concurrent pregnancies. This means there are embryos of two different ages in the uteri. This is called superfoetation and, although it happens only rarely, is no less amazing for all that.

Ancient or modern?

Rabbits and hares are unusual mammals in that they adopt a parenting strategy called 'absenteeism' in which they show minimal care of their young. Rabbits are even odder because, additionally, when born their babies are very undeveloped and helpless. This state is common enough amongst the mammalia, but, in other species, it is associated with a great deal of care from one or both parents. This is clearly demonstrated by the mother cat who makes a nest for her young, cleans them, stimulates them to urinate, curls up with them to keep them warm, retrieves them back to the nest if they wander and generally acts as a major life support system. This type of care is known as the 'shelter system' and is about as different as you can get from the absentee style of care shown by rabbits. So where does this difference come from and why should the rabbit be so unusual? Here we enter the realm of disagreement and speculation.

Disagreement because there are two differing views of the origin of the absentee system of care. The first hypothesis proposes that it represents a very early system of parental care. In contrast, the second hypothesis suggests that the early system was the shelter system and the absenteeism is more recent and is a derivation of the older system. Both these stances remain speculative, because as yet, there is no way of obtaining hard evidence with which to test the evolutionary origins of this behaviour pattern.

It is generally accepted that the ancestors of living mammals gave birth to young who were 'altricial', that is, born in an undeveloped state. These youngsters would be born with their eyes and ears closed and non-functional, neither teeth nor fur and thus would be unlikely to be able to maintain their body temperature for very long. Indeed many mammals from insectivores to carnivores are born in such a state.

Given that the young of the first mammals were like this, then their parents must have developed some degree of parental care else the young would surely die. At the very least, this would have involved nursing and the use of a pouch or nest, the latter becoming mandatory when the litter weight became so big as to impair the foraging efficiency of the parent. Whether other aspects of parental care, such as grooming and retrieval of the young, which are major features of the shelter system, had developed by this stage of mammalian evolution is unknown. If not, then the use of the nest site which is separate from the parents' resting site, as employed by the rabbit, may merely have been the first step in the evolution of parental care.

It has also been suggested that primitive behaviours will be observed in species that are anatomically primitive. Certainly the lagomorphs have characteristics, such as the location of the scrotum in front of the penis, which have led them to be considered as primitive, that is, ancient, members of the mammalian order. This then lends partial support to the hypothesis that absenteeism is an early form of care. But why isn't it seen in other orders, such as the *Insectivora*, which are also judged to be anatomically primitive? Similarly, it does not necessarily follow that having a primitive behaviour or anatomical characteristic means that the species itself is primitive. It may mean that the species has retained that characteristic either because it is still useful or there has been no pressure to remove it. After all, we humans still have an, albeit non-functional, appendix and are not considered to be primitive. So, on to the second hypothesis.

This hypothesis suggests that absenteeism is a specialization in response to certain environmental pressures acting on the species. It implies that the adaptive strategy involved a reduction in parental behaviour from a more complex system such as the shelter system. What would be a strong enough pressure to cause such a reduction, which in turn increases the survival rate of the species? Well, one candidate is predation.

As we have seen rabbits are very highly predated and not only from outside. For, should a female rabbit discover a nest of babies which are not her own she has no hesitation in killing them. As far as external predators are concerned, rabbits are not very good at defending themselves, preferring rapid retreat as the major means of escape. By hiding their young away from prying eyes and visiting them only infrequently, rabbit mothers can reduce the chances of their young being found by a hungry fox or other female.

This argument is fine as far as it goes, but it doesn't yet answer the question of whether absenteeism is primitive or not. One possible source of evidence would be to see whether rabbits show any bits of behaviour which are usually associated with the shelter system. It is only a possible source of evidence because it can always be argued that these behaviours are a recent evolutionary development rather than being remnants of an older system.

My own work has shown that, given the right circumstances, rabbits do occasionally indulge in unrabbit-like behaviours such as grooming their young. Of course, the arguments and evidence are more complex than my outline here. There are other factors to be considered, for example, what about hares, who give birth to highly developed young, not a primitive characteristic? When all is weighed up, my own conclusion is in favour of the second hypothesis. Namely, absenteeism, as we see it in the lago-morphs, represents a specific adaptation to predation pressures, and has been evolved by a reduction in the parental care as typified by the older, shelter system. Of course, you may disagree and prefer the alternative explanation. Whichever you support, it still remains that in terms of their parental behaviour rabbits are very unusual and very interesting.

Babies grow up

Baby hares and rabbits are quite, quite different. Baby hares are born as miniatures of their parents. Weighing 100g (3·5oz) (as compared to the adult size of approximately 3000g/6·5lb), they come into the world equipped with a full coat of fur. Their eyes see clearly, their ears and noses are fully functional and, after a short period of getting used to their legs, they can run swiftly and surely.

Rabbit kittens are virtually the complete opposite. A newborn rabbit does not look remotely like an adult. At birth it weighs only 30g (1oz), whereas its parents weigh about 1500g (3·3lb). With tiny, almost useless

January	February	March	April
Rabbit breeding season starts: 20-40% of does pregnant. Peak damage to early crops by hares.	First rabbit litters born (4-6 litters, on average, in a good season). Pest control hare shoots. Breading season starts in mid-month.	90% of rabbit does pregnant. Spring moult starts. End of hunting (coursing and beagling) season. First hare litters born at end of month.	90% of does pregnant and lactating. Hares breeding. Hare meat not allowed to be sold between March and July.
May	**June**	**July**	**August**
Breeding season still in full-swing for both species. Hares will have 3 litters in a good season.	Breeding season ends for most rabbit populations. Spring moult finishes for both species.	Last rabbit litters weaned. Hares breeding.	Breeding season ends in low density popns. Dispersal of juvenile rabbits born early in season. Hares breeding and moult starting.
September	**October**	**November**	**December**
Early myxomatosis outbreaks. Hare breeding season ends. Crops are harvested.	Rabbit moult begins. Hare hunting season starts. End of moult.	Rabbits, especially young, suffer myxomatosis outbreaks. Potential starvation period for hares on arable land.	End of rabbit moult. Winter crops start to grow providing hares with seasonal food.

The rabbit year.

legs, an extraordinarily long back, a head that seems far too large, and a pink body totally devoid of any fur, the kitten looks like an alien creature. Their eyes are undeveloped and remain closed for 10 days and their small ears are pressed close to their heads and are not functional for some 7 days. Only their noses are in relatively good working order at birth. But by the time they emerge from the nest, they have altered dramatically, both physically and behaviourally. Much of the following description of rabbit development, especially of their very early life, comes from studies (including my own) of domestic rabbits, because it is extremely difficult to study wild nestling rabbits without the mother deserting them, and to my knowledge has never been done. But it is extremely unlikely that the development of domestic and wild rabbits differs in any major way.

The two major problems for newborn rabbit kittens are to keep warm and to be in the right place at the right time to receive their daily feed of milk. For the first week or so the kittens live by a very stereotyped (that is, set) daily routine which has evolved precisely to cope with these two problems.

Just after having been nursed by their mother, all the kittens urinate at the surface of the nest. In this rabbits are unusual, for, unlike other mammals born in an undeveloped state (like mice and dogs), rabbits do not need to be stimulated to urinate by their mother licking their genitals. This simultaneous urination by the kittens immediately after nursing ensures that no single kitten need leave the warmth of the group to urinate, and by urinating on the surface the kittens do not have to rest on damp bedding. For, within 15 minutes, the kittens have completely disappeared by burrowing down into the warm nest of grass and fur.

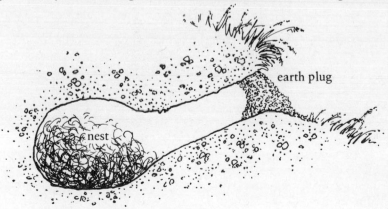

earth plug

nest

Rabbit nest stop.

There they stay, tightly grouped together, in the warmest part of the nest. Newborn rabbits can detect differences in temperatures of as little as 0·2°C. The only movement now is a slow but continual up and down motion of the group as those on the top of the heap of kittens get cool and burrow down through their brothers and sisters to get to the warmer spots below. After about 22 hours of this the whole group gradually becomes more active, slowly working its way up to the surface of the nest, where they will be exposed and thus within easier reach of their mother for nursing.

At the surface, the kittens remain fairly active, gently milling around each other, their heads raised to detect, probably by smell, whether their mother has arrived. Once she does arrive and stands over them, there is a flurry of activity as the kittens jostle to get hold of a nipple. Their heads rapidly move from side to side as their noses seek the object of their desire. The kittens find the nipple using an olfactory cue. The mother secretes a substance which, to baby rabbits anyway, is quite smelly and attractive. The smell gets stronger from her belly towards the nipples and so guides the kittens to the right spot. Having found the nipple, another cue, possibly a different smell, stimulates the kitten to open its mouth and grasp it.

Usually each kitten is firmly attached to a nipple within 20 seconds of the mother's arrival. The kittens do not adopt any particular nursing posture, other than bracing their back legs in an effort to support their ungainly bodies and paddling the mother's body with their front feet in a similar way to a cat treading a person's lap. This treading action of the baby rabbit helps to stimulate the mother to release her milk. In some animals, such as cows, the young suck a reserve of milk from the mother's udder. In others, including the rabbit, the milk is released in a single ejection which occurs after the mother has been sufficiently stimulated by the kittens sucking her nipples and 'treading' her body. This ejection occurs near the end of the nursing episode. The kittens don't stay on just one nipple. Instead, for no clear reason, they jostle for a new position every half-minute or so, some 4-5 changes each nursing visit. The nursing episode lasts about 3 minutes at the end of which the mother, unceremoniously, leaves the young which, after a few seconds of confusion, toddle off to urinate and then go back to sleep in the warmth of the nest.

This routine continues for about a week, after which the young begin to show more interest in their surroundings as their ears begin to function and their eyes begin to open. Also, by now they have started to grow a

Young rabbits about twenty days old, just out of hole.

coat of fur and thus are not so dependent for warmth on the nest lining and the body heat of their littermates. As well as being a bit more active in the nest, the kittens tend not to lie in such a tightly packed group nor spend so much time burrowing underneath each other. After the first week of life the kittens gain more control of their limbs and with this control comes the ability to do more complicated actions such as scratching one's head. Younger kittens look quite silly as they attempt to scratch themselves and more often than not succeed in only scratching the air. When about 12 days old the kittens are quite mobile and can dig and climb a little. At this time it is not unusual, when the mother opens the nest stop, to find that the kittens are no longer in the nest but are waiting just by the entrance and are then nursed above ground.

At about 18 days of age the kittens weigh 150g (5·5oz), more than 5 times as much as they did at birth. Now the mother tends not to plug the entrance to the nest stop so firmly and the young begin to make their first short, tentative excursions into the outside world, scurrying back at any sudden disturbance. By 24 days the young are abandoned by their mother and begin to take part in the general life of the warren. Their skeletons don't stop growing until they are 9 months old and weigh around 900g (nearly 2lb), after which they add weight until they reach their full adult size. Though not fully grown, young rabbits are sexually mature at only 4 months old (when they weigh about 400g/14oz). Young males are unlikely to be able to compete successfully for mates at this age. However, this early maturity means that a female born early in the season may well produce kittens of her own in that same season.

How old is old?

In general, mammals living in the wild tend to have shorter lives than those living in captivity. The rabbit is no exception. A captive rabbit can expect to look forward to a life of 10 years or more but, in the wild, it is an exceptional animal that lives for 5 years. In fact, it is unusual to find a wild rabbit over 2 years old. The main causes of death as a rabbit grows up are drowning, exposure, disease, predation and, of course, predation by man. A similar situation exists for hares. Though research in Poland found one wild, wily specimen of 12, the best a wild British hare can reasonably hope for is a life of only 3 to 4 years.

The most likely time for a rabbit to die is within the first 3 months of its

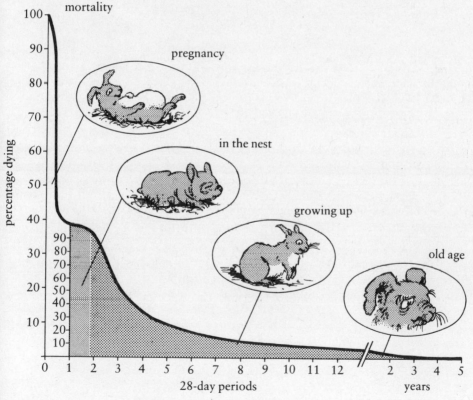

Rabbit mortality at different ages.

life. In most populations 75% of rabbits born will have died by this time and, of the remaining 25%, less than half will live to see their first birthday. Death strikes even the very young. Kittens in the nest are, as we have seen (p.42), very vulnerable to being taken by predators such as fox and badger, or to being orphaned should their mother suffer a similar fate. If the summer is wet, then many will drown as the nest stops become flooded. When they have emerged, the kittens can easily die of exposure in wet, cool weather. With the coming of autumn many youngsters contract myxomatosis from their more resistent elders, and at this time of year their corpses are often to be found. Currently, the number of young that survive their first summer and autumn averages at just over one per adult, thus, generally, there is only a slow rise in the overall number of rabbits across the country, depending on factors such as the weather. There is, however, great variation in rabbit numbers between different localities and also between years for any particular population.

Variation in population numbers is related to many factors. For instance, in light, well drained sandy soils the population will naturally be higher than in the difficult to burrow, easily waterlogged clays and peats. The numbers of predators, weather conditions and the action of man, both directly as in gassing for pest control and shooting of rabbits for sport, and, indirectly, the destruction of hedgerows and habitat all affect the population.

Even amongst those animals over a year old the death rate is very high. Anything between 50–80% of a local population may die each year. So, on average, a single population is made up of totally new individuals every 2 years. For male rabbits an early death is even more likely than it is for females. Males tend to be out away from the safety of the burrow more often than females, either patrolling their territory or living away from the warren as satellites. Thus, they are more exposed than females to dangers such as predation. This increased probability of death is reflected in the make-up of the average rabbit population where, though roughly equal numbers of males and females are born, the adult proportions are nearer 3 females to 2 males.

Rabbits and the landscape

Rabbits are, and have been for at least 200 years, Britain's most important mammalian mowing machine. Eating mostly grasses, they are very selective feeders. They choose only the more nutritious varieties from the many available species of wild grasses and herbage and from the agricultural cereals and cultivated grasses. Poisonous, thorny or generally distasteful plants such as ragwort, bramble, stinging nettles and bracken are left alone and thus tend to grow in profusion near burrows. Grasses are a most desirable food because of their resistance to grazing pressure; that is, they grow continuously despite being chomped regularly. While most mammals find grass a problem to digest because of its unusually thick cell walls, the rabbit's digestive system admirably overcomes this problem. In winter, when grasses are not so readily available, rabbits will browse the lower leaves and shoots of trees. If hard pressed, as when the ground is covered in snow, they will do untold damage by stripping the bark off trees.

The rabbit habit of feeding near its home causes intensive pressure on the local (palatable) flora. Changes in agricultural methods and the persecution of predators by gamekeepers between the 1800s and the arrival of myxomatosis in the 1950s, allowed rabbit numbers to increase dramatically. There were an estimated 100 million of them in Britain just before myxomatosis. So many rabbits nibbling away obviously had an effect on crops and on the natural flora and fauna. Nonetheless, the ramifications of the rabbit appetite on the landscape were not really appreciated until the population was so swiftly devastated by myxomatosis.

The elimination of virtually all rabbits in the 1950s meant that young trees and seedlings were no longer destroyed and woodlands were able to regenerate. Herbs and grasses were left to grow to their full height and flower. Plant successions took place, causing some small plants and annuals to become extinct locally as they were overshadowed by their larger neighbours. Areas which, pre-myxomatosis, had supported a wide variety of plants became dominated by a few species of grass and shrub. For example, the effect of rabbits' decline on chalk downlands was to cause the demise of many of Britain's orchid species which previously had flourished in the short turf conditions maintained by rabbit grazing. As ever in ecological issues the situation was not simple. A good example of the complexity is the effect of myxomatosis on ragwort. Rabbits tend not to eat ragwort and its presence around rabbit burrows is common. Myxomatosis, by killing the rabbits, removed any grazing pressure there may have been. This allowed the ragwort to complete its life cycle, but the seeds did not germinate. It appears that the seeds needed the eroded soil surface, caused by rabbit digging. Within three years of the disappearance of the rabbit, ragwort was superseded and replaced by other plants.

The increase in the height of grasses has been to the advantage of many invertebrate species. The shelter of the long grass means that the micro-climate of the lower vegetation is more stable, benefitting snails and woodlice amongst others. The tall stems give resting places for many insects away from hot or damp conditions. They provide attachment sites for the pupa of moths such as the six-spot burnet and anchoring sites for the webs of spiders.

On the other hand, some species did not fare so well and, in one case at least — that of the large blue butterfly — myxomatosis spelt direct habitat loss and extinction. The eggs of this butterfly are laid, almost exclusively, in the buds of wild thyme, one egg per bud. Here the larva hatches after about a week and proceeds to feed on the flowers of the thyme (and any other larvae it happens to come across). After the second moult the larva drops off the plant and soon is found by a member of the ant genus Myrmica. These ants act like cowherds and proceed to 'milk' the larva's honey gland. In return for this delicacy, the ant picks up the larva and takes it back to the ant nest. Though not essential to the ant's survival, butterfly larva honey is obviously highly prized. For, in return for being repeatedly milked while in the nest, the larva is fed on the ant's own larvae until it is full grown. Then it is left to hibernate in the nest until the spring when it again eats ant larvae, finally pupating and emerging from the ant nest as a fully grown large blue butterfly. Unfortunately for the large blue, the host species of ant only lives in sward which is less than 1cm in height. This is common enough where rabbits are feeding, but the post-myxomatosis increase in grass height meant that there was no longer a suitable habitat for the ant. Though other hosts were available for the butterfly larvae, these were not ideal and by 1979 the large blue was extinct in this country.

Some vertebrates too suffered from the changes rendered by the arrival of myxomatosis. One loser was the sand lizard. This lizard needs rabbit grazing and digging to expose areas of loose sand in which it can lay its eggs. The reduction of such suitable breeding sites has inevitably led to a reduction in the population of these lizards.

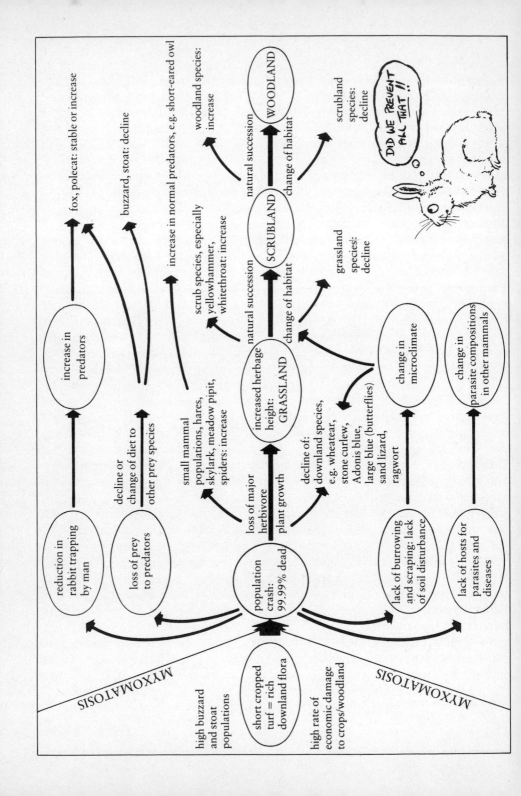

The rabbit, being both a herbivore and an important prey species, has a complex relationship to other prey species. While competing for available food resources with other prey species, its presence, especially when abundant, also reduces the predator pressure on these other prey species. The removal of the rabbit and consequent increase in vegetation height, number of seeds and amount of long tussocky grass meant that there were more suitable habitats and more food for many smaller mammals such as the short-tailed vole. The subsequent rise in numbers of these and other seed-eaters resulted in much damage being done to forest nurseries. Indeed, plague levels of these small mammals occurred in the first 2–3 years after myxomatosis. However, the small mammals, like the mice and voles, also suffered an increase in predation as many predators switched from a mainly rabbit to a mainly vole or mouse diet. Because of the high plague levels of prey, some predators had exceptionally good breeding years. Short-eared owls were numerous in the winter of 1956–7, and fox vixens, having fed well all winter on voles, were in such good breeding condition that litters of up to 10 cubs were recorded, instead of the usual 3 or 4. The weasel, too, responded favourably, with record numbers being noted in 1957. Though vole numbers soon dropped from these plague levels, they remained much higher than when the rabbits had also been abundant. Numbers began to fall in the 1960s when the rabbits started to make their comeback.

Not all predators were able to switch easily from a mostly rabbit diet and some species suffered directly from the reduction in the availability of their favourite prey. The stoat was probably the most dependent on the rabbit, which comprised over 80% of its diet. Though this predator did change its habits, hunting grey squirrels and eating the usually shunned moles and shrews, it seems these adaptations were insufficient to maintain the stoat population. It is only since the 1960s, with the increase in rabbits, that the stoat population too has increased.

More indirectly, the reduction in rabbits has favoured a relative of the stoat, namely the polecat. Since myxomatosis, the range of the polecat has increased; it is now found in most areas of Wales and the border counties. Able to take advantage of other prey species, the polecat has also benefitted from the cessation of commercial rabbit trapping (especially gin-trapping) which occurred after myxomatosis. Polecats were often a non-target victim of the trapper's catch.

The impact of myxomatosis on buzzards was twofold and severe: for

(Opposite) *Indirect effects of myxomatosis on the landscape.*

Buzzard with rabbit prey.

the adult bird, the rabbits had constituted a significant part of their diet. The drastic fall in rabbit numbers led to under-nourished birds which in turn led to fewer eggs being laid. But worse was to follow. The diet of young nestling buzzards is composed almost exclusively of rabbits. The outcome was that the adult birds, after myxomatosis, had fewer young and were less able to feed the reduced number they had. The situation was only made worse by gamekeepers who, fearing for their pheasants, increased their activities against the buzzard. One population of buzzards which had regularly produced 28–33 chicks a season pre-myxomatosis, reared none in 1955 and only 7 in 1956.

Other birds were affected, not so much by the loss of food as by the loss of habitat. The peregrine falcon needs cliffs on which to nest and open ground over which to hunt – which was the pre-myxomatosis character of the South Downs. The fall in rabbit numbers and the associated rise in vegetation height are probably significant causes of the disappearance of this bird from the area.

Other frequenters of downland habitats, the wheatear, lapwing and stone curlew, already had to cope with habitat loss due to afforestation and cultivation. Myxomatosis meant a further reduction in population as the height of downland vegetation rose from 1–2cm to 15–20cm. Conversely, the skylark and meadow pipit probably benefitted from the thickening of the grassland.

The arrival of myxomatosis and the consequent fall in rabbit numbers resulted in major changes in the British landscape, some of which may mean there is now less habitat available for rabbit recolonization. This will of course limit the rabbit's increase. However, rabbit numbers are increasing significantly (and, incidentally, while still a relatively common animal with an estimated population of several million, hare numbers are decreasing). The rabbit is still a major agricultural pest and further steps need to be taken in order to control and limit its comeback which, if allowed unchecked, would have further and different long-term effects on our landscape.

Hunters and conservation

Hunting, with its association with primitive feelings of blood lust, which our civilized world would rather forget, is a topic surrounded by controversy and strong emotions. Where people stand in relation to the issue is a personal matter and not one that I propose to tackle here. Suffice it to say that in the present atmosphere of intensive farming which, as well as producing infamous grain surpluses, also destroys vast tracts of natural habitat, it can be argued justifiably that the hunting lobby has an important role to play in the conservation of hares.

Rabbits are not considered much of a game animal in Britain but the hare ranks close behind grouse, pheasant and partridge in the list of preferred small game. Unlike shooting game birds, the thrill for the hare hunters is the chase and specifically the opportunity to watch dogs at work. The hare makes an ideal quarry because it escapes over open

Hare coursing with lurchers.

country, and is thus highly visible, is fast and has considerable stamina. There are two different types of hare hunting: beagling and coursing.

Beagling is where the hare is hunted by packs of beagles, the breed of Snoopy fame. The dogs either flush out a hare or follow its scent. Beagles are slow dogs and the hunt is followed on foot. Though slow, these dogs have a good measure of stamina and perseverance and they catch their quarry by simply wearing it down (though there are many stories where they are outwitted by a fresh hare taking the lead from an exhausted one). In fact, more often than not the hunt ends without a kill, and beagling contributes little to hare mortality. This may be just as well since beaglers often prefer areas with a low population as the scent of too many hares tends to confuse the dogs.

In contrast, coursing requires a high population of hares. Coursing is a knock-out event between a pair of dogs, usually greyhounds. The object is not to kill but for each dog to score against its opponent in leading the chase and initiating manoeuvres such as changing direction. Basically, the track is a field of grass or stubble which joins onto another in which many hares are known to lie up. Concealed along the joining edge is the dog handler, the 'slipper'. The hares are flushed out of the field, preferably one at a time, by a semi-circle of beaters. If the hare is adult and healthy, the slipper slips the two dogs from their leads when he judges the hare has been given an adequate start. Once having crossed to the other end of the coursing field the hares can slip out of sight into a hedge or fence, at which point the dogs, who hunt by sight, give up the chase. At formal coursing events only about 20% of hares that run are killed.

As formal hare coursers require a high hare population they have been a force for the conservation of the species and its habitat, encouraging farmers to leave stubble as winter fodder, to limit the use of chemicals and to desist from hare shoots organized on grounds of pest control. Unfortunately, the growing trend for unorganized coursing events, basically poaching, has the opposite effect. Many people now own greyhound crossbreeds, or lurchers, and sadly a large number cannot resist the temptation of seeing their dogs work. This would be fine if they joined an organized club but illicit coursing affects the hares in two ways. Firstly, there are those animals killed directly. Secondly, and perhaps more importantly, they make many farmers decide that having a hare population encourages trespassers. The obvious solution, from the farmer's point of view, is to get rid of the hares.

Bye baby bunting

For generations rabbits have formed a welcome addition to the diet of many people. Though legally the property of the landowner, rabbits were not uncommon on the tables of the more lowly inhabitants of these isles. The wily poacher had various assistants, not least being the ferret. The ferret also played a more legal role as a tool of the warrener-cum-gamekeeper. Where predators were controlled in order to protect game-birds, rabbit numbers had to be controlled by other means, one of which was the ferret.

The ferret has been a domestic associate of man for some 2,500 years. It is descended from the Steppe Polecat and is of the same family as the rabbit's arch enemies, the stoats and weasels. The ferret was domesticated in order to help man provide food for his family and, originally, it would have been used to hunt creatures such as European marmots. These

Ferreting.

animals live in colonies similar to those of rabbits with underground burrow systems, but they are substantially bigger with average weights of 4–8kg (8–17lb), a reasonable size catch by anyone's standard. It is only comparatively recently that ferrets were brought to England to work rabbits and provide a tasty meal, maybe all the more tasty for having been obtained with a degree of legal risk. Nowadays, it is not necessary to have a ferret to help support your family. However, many people, both rural and urban, enjoy both the opportunity of working closely with these bright, friendly animals and the rewards of that co-operation.

Hunting rabbits with ferrets calls for a division of labour. The ferret's job is to chase the rabbits out of the burrows and the man's is to catch and dispatch them. Having found a suitable warren, and obtained permission from the landowner, the ferreter covers all the holes with nets. The ferret is then shown an entrance and left to proceed of its own accord down the labyrinth. If the warren is occupied, then soon rabbits will appear in the nets and the ferreter will have to work fast if he is not to lose a good number of his prey who, given half a chance, will be off out of the net and away.

Hunting with ferrets takes place during the winter months. There are several reasons why summer is not suitable, all of which are related to the presence of baby rabbits. Firstly, a female rabbit is quite likely to turn and defend her offspring. In the confines of the burrow there is little room for escape and a hefty kick from a rabbit can do a lot of harm to a ferret. Also, after such treatment, an inexperienced ferret may be put off the whole idea and no longer be of any use as a hunting companion. Secondly, if the doe should bolt, then the deserted young, especially if still nestbound, comprise a tasty snack for the ferret. After indulging itself, the ferret will probably curl up and sleep off the effects of this unexpected treat. Meanwhile, its owner has either to await above ground, or decide to dig out his errant companion, not the most alluring prospect in warm weather. One way to avoid this happening is to take the edge off the ferret's appetite before work starts. However, in such an eventuality, experienced ferreters will often attach a 'bad-tempered' ferret to a line, or long leash, and send him down to flush out his dining predecessor. But such a practice is full of potential danger as the line can get tangled on roots and rocks, possibly strangling the poor ferret.

If you are interested in keeping and working ferrets, then please read around the subject further, and ask advice from other ferret owners.

Rabbit control

For centuries, up until the advent of myxomatosis, many people earned their living with gin traps and snares from the trapping of wild rabbits. Even after the Second World War around 40 million rabbit carcases a year were traded for their meat and fur. However, the income from this trade in no way offset the losses caused by the rabbit damage to crops and woodland. The density of the British rabbit population in the first half of this century cost the nation's farmers, horticulturalists and foresters over £50 million per annum (equivalent to some £250 million in today's prices). In contrast, the carcase trade only recouped £15 million of which a mere £2 million found its way back into agriculture. The cost to the nation was, in part, due to direct damage to crops and, additionally, due to the cost of the counter measures taken to eliminate or exclude the rabbit from these vulnerable agricultural areas.

The first wave of myxomatosis eliminated over 99% of the rabbit population. However, the rabbit has steadily recovered its numbers and the present nationwide population is about 20% of the pre-myxomatosis level and in some areas, notably the south-east, rabbit numbers are nearly back to their former pest levels. The annual damage was estimated in 1986 to have cost Britain between £90–120 million. It is believed that this figure may rise to £400 million within a few years. It is not surprising that, with the disappointment of myxomatosis, farmers are looking for a new final solution.

It is unlikely that there will be one. It is more realistic to assume that the rabbit menace is only going to be kept at bay by a concerted effort on all fronts using a variety of methods. The Ministry of Agriculture, Fisheries and Food (MAFF) is the government body concerned with the agricultural welfare of our country. It employs scientists, some of whom are involved in research into the rabbit problem. There are several options of pest control available which could be developed or improved and which could act to support each other.

At present, the most effective form of control is gassing, using hydrogen cyanide. While it certainly kills rabbits, its use also involves local destruction of thickets and hedgerows in order that the pest controllers can get to the burrows. There are many areas which do not have much in the way of hedgerows but certainly have an increasing rabbit problem. In such places gassing is likely to be most effective without causing concern to conservationists who, rightly, wish to protect hedgerow habitats.

Poison bait is a possible future means of rabbit control. Although at present rabbit poisoning is illegal it is quite probable that, should the rabbit problem become too great, this law would be changed. Unfortunately, the use of poisons has many drawbacks. In an ideal world (from the farmers', not the rabbits' point of view) there would be a poison available which would have the following attributes: it would only affect rabbits, it would be humane, it would be lethal in one dose so it didn't have to sit about in fields for more than one night and it would break down quickly in the victim's body, thereby not causing secondary poisoning to any animal which proceeded to dine on the unfortunate rabbit's carcase. Sadly, no such poison is available, nor, as yet, are there funds to enable scientists to develop one. Given that, researchers are investigating ways in which existing poisons can be given to rabbits with the minimum risk to other animals. This has involved a lot of work into the feeding behaviour of rabbits and how to make the bait (carrots) more attractive. Tests have been conducted using carrots which have been doused in rabbit odours from gland secretions and urine. Although such odours are attractive to rabbits, they still preferred to eat untreated carrots!

There are some disturbing issues relating to the possibility of the use of poisons as a major form of rabbit control. First, there is the question of abuse. Unfortunately, no matter how stringent the laws concerning usage may be, abuse of chemicals is common, as regrettably has been shown with the previous use of agricultural herbicides and pesticides. Secondly, if a presently available poison, which is not rabbit specific, is used, then there is the important question of other animals being affected. While poison on or in a carrot bait is intended for rabbits, there is no doubt that the bait is also attractive to other species such as shrews, slugs and deer. Predators too are at risk from eating contaminated prey. Finally, work in Western Australia has already shown that poisons may only be effective in the short term. To begin with the poison used killed a lot of rabbits (and predators), but there were survivors. These were the rabbits that were predisposed to be frightened of novel objects – such as stacks of (poisoned) carrots. Soon a whole new generation of rabbits grew up that wouldn't touch the bait – thus defeating the object of the exercise.

There are other means of control – some tried and tested, others still awaiting development. Ministry scientists have investigated the effectiveness of varying heights and designs of electric and rabbit-proof fencing. Their results when applied have reduced farmers' fencing costs by 30%

and rabbit damage to protected crops by as much as 80%.

Traditional methods of control, that is, ferreting and shooting, have also benefitted from research. It has been shown that 30% more females (potential or actual breeders) than males can be taken from burrows by ferrets and that this form of control is most effective in winter. Similarly, rabbit shooting in winter has a greater effect on the population than at any other time of the year. Easing up on the shooting of predators may also benefit the farmer. Predators can significantly contribute to rabbit control, especially in areas where rabbit numbers are already low. It is not surprising that there is a positive relationship between the number of gamekeepers and the numbers of rabbits in a given area.

Biological control methods offer new avenues of hope for rabbit infested farmland. American studies have shown that some plants protect their buds from grazing (by hares) by producing an unpalatable toxin. It may well be that some plants are equally untasty to rabbits. This could be a new strain of crop or a naturally occurring wild grass. If the latter, then a strip of such a grass could be planted around a crop field. As it wouldn't be cropped by rabbits the grass would soon grow (and stay) long. Long grass gets wet and stays wet, and long, wet grass is lethal to newly emerged, young rabbits which easily die of exposure.

Or how about a rabbit contraceptive? Not as far-fetched an idea as might be thought. Research in Cambridgeshire has found that rabbits produce a hormone in response to the shorter days of autumn. This

hormone switches off the sex drive in male rabbits and triggers the contraction of the testicles so reducing sperm production. If this hormone could be administered to wild rabbits at the beginning of the breeding season then there could be a reduction in the number of kittens born. Similarly, other work has shown that some plants contain specific acids that inhibit breeding in some herbivores. If one could be isolated that affected rabbits only, then baits containing this acid could artificially reduce the breeding of rabbits.

None of the methods outlined – the continuing effects of disease (especially myxomatosis), gassing, ferreting, shooting and biological controls (including the rabbit 'pill') – are likely to be in themselves the final solution. More likely, only a combination of tactics will yield good control. The complete extinction of rabbits would not be advisable – not only for emotional reasons but because, as we have seen, the rabbit exerts an important influence on both the plants it does (and doesn't) eat and on the wild animals with which it shares its habitat. However, on the grounds of economics alone, its numbers cannot be allowed to return to pre-myxomatosis levels. It is going to take a concerted, co-ordinated effort on the part of farmers, government, conservationists and scientists to ensure that the rabbit is controlled, hopefully in a humane, ecologically safe and economic manner.

Mr McGregor's garden

I'm sure many a British gardener has great sympathy for Mr McGregor as they too witness the effects of the rabbit's rapacious appetite. What is worse is that, unlike Peter Rabbit, real rabbits do not restrict their activities merely to the vegetable plot. So can the keen gardener do more than vainly brandish his rake, McGregor style, at the retreating white scuts? The answer is yes, though of course there is no guarantee that any measure will completely prevent the determined rabbit from sampling the products of your hard work.

An obvious solution is to enclose your garden with rabbit-proof fencing. Whether you would consider this a realistic option is likely to depend on the size of your garden and the extent of rabbit infestation. A traditional, and cheaper, way is to circle your plot with prickly dried gorse or holly leaves. A border of rue is also suggested and will make a delightful addition to your herb stocks.

Another means of deterring

rabbits is to use one of the commercially available animal repellents. These products are designed to dissuade grazing by the application of chemicals which rabbits perceive as smelling and/or tasting horrible. Some people seem to find these very effective deterrents, others are not so convinced. Older 'smelly' remedies are based on the observations of country folk. Noting that rabbits tend to leave grass around cow pats well alone, they recommend spraying the area with the juice from cow manure. Apparently, human urine works just as well.

Finally, you could always base your show on plants that rabbits naturally tend to avoid. A display of snowdrops and daffodils can herald a rabbit-free spring in your garden. Flowers such as yellow flag, cyclamen, scarlet pimpernel and foxglove create a riot of colour. Set against a backdrop of clematis or rhododendron and balanced by the tranquil shades of box and laurel the imaginative gardener can produce an exceptional garden, pleasing to the eye and uninviting to the rabbit. The more alternative gardeners amongst us will be pleased to know that rabbits do not share their enthusiasm for the cannabis plant.

If you are planning a rabbit-proof display then it is worthwhile seeking advice from your local horticultural society. One general rule of thumb is that rabbits tend to avoid berry-producing plants.

Rabbit farming

Not all farmers dislike rabbits. Some positively encourage them onto their land, investing time and money in their welfare. But there is a subtle difference – the rabbits so favoured are domestic, not wild, and are kept caged in large buildings.

Over 1,500 farmers in Britain breed rabbits as a crop. Between them they produce some 7 million kilos of meat annually, giving a turnover of over £20 million. In recent years, for various reasons, including their desire for foreign currency, the Chinese have been selling rabbit meat to the British consumer at a lower price than the British farmer has been able to. Thus, most home-produced meat, not sold at the farm gate, is exported to Europe and elsewhere. These sales make up the bulk of the annual revenue.

It is not just the carcase that produces an income. Rabbit pelts are used in the manufacture of glues and fertilizers. In Britain there is no longer any substantial trade in fur. However, up until the 1950s there was a major trade in rabbit pelts. They were used to make felt for hats as well as being dried and treated for use in articles of clothing. While much fur was imported, a large number of home-grown rabbit pelts were prepared and dyed in British factories for the clothing industry. To make a single full-length coat required the pelts from at least 40 rabbits. In the days when high fashion meant wearing fur, rabbit-skin clothes were in great demand as, unlike other furs, they were within reach of most people's pockets.

The guts and offal of the rabbits are removed when the carcase is cleaned at the meat factory. These are then incorporated into animal feedstuffs – especially for mink, fish at fish farms and pet foods.

Even the dung has a commercial value as it has a high nitrogen content and helps make excellent compost. The best method for turning dung into compost is through the action of worms. Indeed, if you have a compost heap a brief exploration will reveal an army of them busily at work. Worms are also put to work on a commercial basis. Worm farmers breed angling worms for use as fishing bait or in high grade protein feeds for poultry and fish farms. While growing and breeding, the worms are kept on beds of rabbit dung off which they happily feed, turning it into compost which is then sold to the horticultural industry. Though there are less than a dozen worm farms in the country, British worm technology provides a convenient outlet for rabbit manure, which instead of merely being dumped can usefully be returned to the land.

There are some other odd commercial uses for lagomorph parts. Many horticulturalists believe that a rabbit tail is the best tool for the artificial pollination of flowers. Hares' feet are held in high esteem by dentists and goldsmiths for their furry padding. Dentists use them to sprinkle the French chalk required in the manufacture of dentures, while goldsmiths use them to sweep up precious gold dust when making jewellery.

Another major commercial outlet for rabbits is for use in research. Rabbits are bred at farms which have been approved by the government, along guidelines laid down by the Universities Federation for Animal Welfare. Research rabbit farms supply about 60% of rabbits used in research. The rest are bred by the laboratories themselves which thereby gain the additional, and often necessary, knowledge of the animals' genetic heritage and environmental history.

Farmers and hare conservation

Farmers are unlikely ever to be supporters of the wild rabbit, but their argument against the hare is less bitter. On the whole farmers tend to ignore (or be less aware of) damage to their crops caused by hares. Not so blatant as rabbits, hares tend to move about in the middle of fields leaving little patches of grazed areas which can easily pass unnoticed when the crop is viewed from the edge. Traditionally, arable farmers also consider the hare to be the herald of wildlife on the farm and the combination of these two factors means that, in general, farmers are benevolently inclined towards this species. Of course, if they feel that their land (and pockets) are supporting too many hares, they will not hesitate to organize hare shoots.

Hare shoots are usually held in February. A group of fields is surrounded by a cordon of people armed with shotguns. Slowly, the people move inwards, driving the hares before them into the centre. The hares are shot as they try to escape. Up to 60% of the population can be quickly dealt with in this way, though a vigorous population will soon recover and where hares are abundant shoots will occur annually. However, where the population is low and not very productive, perhaps as a result of modern intensive farming methods, then a hare shoot can easily wipe it out completely.

Unfortunately, the sad fact is that hare numbers are declining in this country. Hares, unlike foxes for example, have not adapted to survive in urban areas, nor do they live in woodlands and, unfortunately, most nature reserves are too small to support viable populations. The future of the hare depends heavily upon the actions of the farming community. Of course, as in every other area of conservation, any measures taken will only be temporary if, in consequence, they hurt someone's (in this case the farmer's) pocket. And so long as arable farms are turning into food factories, then there will be no place for the hare. However, it appears that the tide is turning and farmers are being encouraged by the public and government to provide for wildlife as well as the nation's bellies.

So how can farmers help the hare? Hares need food and, to some extent, cover. In order to increase the number of hares the availability of these two resources must be increased.

Of greatest importance is a food supply available throughout the year. Hares do not lay down much in the way of fat deposits and consequently even a short period without food will quickly lead to starvation. However, just because a field is green does not mean a hare can live off it. Hares need short growing crops and fields full of grown cereals are of no use, unless there is also an abundance of weeds.

The more traditional farming methods, where fields were small and crops were rotated, provided an ideal habitat – a patchwork landscape through which the hare never had to travel far to find food. In such a system food was available all year round. In winter and early spring wheat was growing, and by late spring, when the wheat was too tall, the spring barley would provide an alternative. From mid-summer to mid-winter, when all cereal crops were too tall to be palatable or had been harvested, ley meadows were rich in grasses and herbs.

By contrast, modern farming methods are not so suitable. Large fields of a single crop mean the hares have to travel far for food. Crop rotation is

Brown hare in stubble field.

no longer common practice, meaning that harvest, the time of plenty for humans, is often the time of want for hares. The farmer reaps his crop in the late summer, leaving nothing for the hare until the winter cereals begin to emerge in November. Many individuals do not survive this period. Farmers could easily alter this situation. Fields that are not to be sown until the spring could be left as stubble until late winter. Stubble is a rich source of wild herbs and grasses which can keep a hare plump during the lean time. Short grasses supply another useful stop-gap, as, for example, when in long strips, to be used as horse gallops between fields. These should preferably consist of both annual and perennial grasses as well as clovers.

Cover protects animals from the worst of the weather, providing shade in the summer and shelter in winter. Small areas of hedgerows, shelter belts and rough banks distributed around the farm will amply suffice for the hare.

The above measures should reduce the number of deaths due to natural causes. A well dispersed and continuous supply of food will help keep disease at bay, while shelter will help the hares avoid predators.

Hares can also be helped by a sympathetic attitude on the part of the farmer as he carries out his jobs. For example, potentially lethal activities, like grass cutting and stubble burning, should be carried out in such a way as to allow hares a decent opportunity to escape. Spraying with lethal herbicides, if done on a dry morning, will cause fewer deaths than if done in the dampness of the evening just as hares are about to begin feeding.

Farmers determine much of how our wildlife fares. The above practical measures plus incentives, such as subsidies, could ensure that farmers will be able to afford to take a more protective, benevolent attitude to conservation.

Rabbits in research

Scientists who work with animals can be divided arbitrarily into those who work mainly in the field and those who work mainly in laboratories. Investigations using wild animals tend to be confined to the field. This is partly because most of these studies are, at least indirectly, concerned with the behaviour of the animal, and the behaviour of a wild animal is best studied in the wild. One good example is the enormous amount of field work that has been done on rabbit behaviour by scientists developing pest control measures. These workers often spend long cold nights observing the behaviour of their study animal and employ various pieces of technology such as radio-tracking collars and night-viewing equipment, as well as pen and paper. Of course, this doesn't mean that field scientists never see the inside of a laboratory. Specimens are brought back for further investigation, such as when detailed laboratory inspection of gut contents and faecal samples is required when investigating rabbit diets. Very little of the scientific research based in laboratories uses captive wild animals. One obvious reason for this is the difficulty of handling and keeping them. Most laboratory work employs domestic breeds.

Animals used in scientific research may be studied in their own right, as in much behavioural research. Alternatively, the animals may merely be a means to an end; a suitable and convenient tool through which phenomena, such as the action of drugs, can be studied. One of the animals most commonly used, after mice and rats, is the domestic rabbit. Approximately 300,000 are used in pure and applied science each year.

The rabbit is a popular research animal thanks to characteristics of its basic biology. It is docile and easily handled. Its size means that it can be conveniently housed – the average size of a laboratory cage is 60 × 60 ×60cm (24 × 24 × 24 inches) (double this if housing a female and her litter). The rabbit's general robustness and feeding habits make it an easy and economical creature to keep. It doesn't require buildings with elaborate heating or ventilation systems and can be healthily maintained on a dry commercial diet of pelleted grass. These factors, combined with its propensity to breed and its rapid growth rate, mean that a regular supply of animals can be kept at a reasonable cost.

The rabbit also possesses several unique characteristics which make it a highly desirable animal for various areas of biological research. For example, it has large and reasonably accessible veins in its ear. These, combined with overall body size, and therefore total volume of blood, enable adequate blood and serum samples to be taken for immunological investigations in medical research. In addition, the rabbit has certain physiological characteristics that seem to be related to resistance or susceptibility to various common human conditions. Thus the rabbit has been widely used in research into the development of treatments for such diseases as arteriosclerosis and tuberculosis. Physiological characteristics that resemble those of man have led to other uses of the rabbit, in addition to those of the drug companies concerned with the development of health aids. One such characteristic is the high degree of sensitivity of the rabbit's skin and eyes to various compounds, reacting in much the same way as human skin and eyes. The consequences of our legal requirements for product testing has meant that many thousands of rabbits have been exploited by the cosmetic industry. Many scientists and people concerned with animal welfare (the two are not mutually exclusive) feel that some of the presently required product tests are outdated and not particularly informative or useful. One of the arguments is that testing products for human use on animals cannot give complete information about how those products will react on people.

Unfortunately, there have been instances in the past, involving both

medical and cosmetic products, which have given testimony to this argument. However, new avenues of research are opening up, as in the use of tissue cultures, and these, combined with a new awareness of the need for animal welfare, are causing changes to be made. One such change is the recent alteration and tightening of the requirements needed before the Home Office will grant an experimental licence. Scientists are legally obliged to hold such a licence prior to carrying out experimental research on animals. There are mixed feelings regarding the new law and what its effect will be on science and on animal welfare. But the fact that it has been given serious consideration, for the first time in nearly a century, is perhaps indicative of our increasing awareness of the world about us, our concern for it and the well-being of its inhabitants. This increase in our consciousness is reflected in an upsurge in the amount of research concerned with what animals are, how they live their lives and why they do the things they do. In these areas of study the rabbit also plays an important role.

The rabbit is a spontaneous ovulator, the female only releasing an egg for fertilization in response to copulation. Consequently, when rabbit breeding is controlled, as in a laboratory, the date of conception can be known accurately. This knowledge is very important to those physiologists, embryologists and even psychologists who are interested in studying reproduction and development.

Biologists are also interested in another aspect of reproduction, namely parental care. Again the rabbit has a great deal to contribute. As we have seen, the form of parental care shown by the lagomorphs is rather unusual, to say the least, and in respect of the rabbit, with its helpless young, it seems to be unique. The variations in parental care across the lagomorph order has great potential for the study of life history tactics, that is, how animals cope with their world. My own work has been concerned with the differences and similarities in the parental behaviours of rabbits and hares, how they are related to their different life styles and predator pressures, and how they might have evolved.

Scientists use different breeds of domestic rabbits depending on their requirements, and they also use different strains. A strain is a particular 'family' of a breed. It's a bit like saying your 'breed' is British, and your 'strain' is Glaswegian, Londoner or whatever. Many strains of rabbit have been developed by inbreeding for the study of particular problems; for example, in order to study human eye problems a strain of rabbit was bred which was prone to developing cataracts in the eyes. Many of these inbred strains are lost when research into that particular topic is discontinued.

Rabbits as pets

Funny big ears, soft fur and liquid eyes set in a friendly round face have made the rabbit irresistible to children of all ages. A stalwart of the soft toy market, the toy rabbit makes an ideal companion for the youngest child, while its size and easy maintenance makes a live domestic rabbit the perfect pet for an older child. In contrast, the hare, which has never been domesticated, has rarely been kept as a pet, a famous exception being the three semi-tame hares kept by the poet Cowper in the 18th century.

Before you get a rabbit, be quite certain you really want a pet: domestic rabbits live for an average of 7 years but frequently this figure is almost doubled. There are some 40 different breeds of domestic rabbit available and it is worth taking time to reflect which would make the most suitable pet for your circumstances. If you do not have a lot of room for your pet it is probably wiser to go for one of the smaller breeds such as the Netherland Dwarf. Alternatively you may have ideas of showing your animal and then it is important to choose a breed that you are really attracted to and can show with genuine pride and interest. My first rabbit, unimaginatively named Thumper, was a Dutch Belted. He always seemed to be immaculately turned out in his best dinner suit of black and white. You might prefer the plush velvet-like coat of a Rex or one of the long-eared Lops.

Whatever you choose, it is important to get your pet while it is young and to handle it frequently and gently, remembering never to pick it up by its ears alone. Frequent handling will get it used to you and make it a much tamer and more rewarding pet. It's not much fun having a pet who, when stroked, cowers, or, worse still, tries to fend you off – a rabbit bite is, believe me, very painful.

Rabbits are fairly hardy beasts and do not require specially heated housing. They will live happily in dry hutches, either in a well ventilated shed or in a sheltered corner of the yard or garden. Of course, they need shelter from draughts, wind and rain and a good bed of straw in which to sleep. I do not suggest that you keep your rabbit in the house; apart from anything else, if given the opportunity it will merrily chomp through books and electric wires.

Rabbits are house-proud beasts in as much as they do not soil their bedding but will establish and keep to a specific toilet area. This is usually well away from the sleeping and feeding areas. So, any hutch must be big

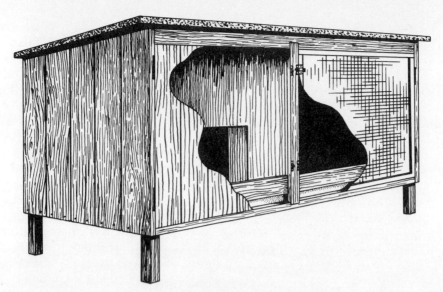

Basic rabbit hutch, with enclosed bedding area (left) and wire-fronted activity area (right).

enough to provide for these three activities: eating, sleeping and toiletting. It is also preferable to have the sleeping area enclosed while the living area should be wire fronted, thus allowing for plenty of fresh air as well as giving your rabbit a view on the world. The cage must also be big enough so that your pet, when full grown, at the very least can stretch out on the floor and high enough so that he can stand at full height on his back legs.

Cages do not have to be bought; a sturdy construction made of wood will suffice. But, be warned, your rabbit will gnaw. Metal cages get over this problem and also make thorough cleaning easier, but they are noisy and tend to be colder. I, or rather my more adept mother, always made my cages out of wood and chicken wire, often using an old tea chest as a foundation.

If you have a garden, then it's pleasurable for your pet and fun for you to let it graze the lawn. A simple wooden frame covered in wire with a lid makes an easily movable 'playpen' in which your rabbit can sit and nibble the grass through the wire floor, without being able to dig holes in the lawn. If the playpen is moved daily around the garden then your rabbit's grazing has the additional advantage of cutting down on the mowing and its droppings act as excellent fertilizer containing a high proportion of nitrogen. Indeed, cage cleanings are a useful addition to the compost heap.

Rabbits are easy and cheap to feed. Water and one of the commercial basic rabbit diets are a must and these can be supplemented with hay and green vegetable peelings from the kitchen. In the spring and summer expeditions to forage for dandelions, groundsel and cow parsley can lead a child into the delights not only of doing something special for its pet, but can also be an introduction to the variety of wild plants available. A few young dandelion leaves, brought home for the rabbit, can easily get side-tracked into a salad for the owners. These wild plants don't only grow in the country but can be found in any piece of city wasteland or, invariably, in the garden flowerbeds.

Pet rabbits tend to lead healthy lives so long as they are fed well, sheltered from the elements and their cages cleaned frequently and regularly. The only routine health care job is clipping their toenails. In the wild these would be worn down by normal activities such as digging but in captivity they must be kept short or else they will make it very painful for the rabbit to walk. Your local vet will clip them for you and, once you know how, this job is easy to do with a good pair of ordinary nail clippers.

Many people all over Britain and from all walks of life keep rabbits, not just as pets but as a competitive hobby. These enthusiasts belong to the little advertised world of the rabbit fancier. Though not given the level of publicity of other show animals, such as dogs, show rabbits are extremely popular, and while not big business in financial terms they certainly have a dedicated following. Exhibiting your rabbit lets you meet and make friends with people who have a common interest. You will probably find there is a local club, or you could join a national club that specializes in your particular breed. If you have any doubts, a visit to the London Championship Show in the autumn, or a glance through any issue of *Fur and Feather*, the official magazine of the British Rabbit Council (BRC), will convince you that rabbit fanciers are professionals in their outlook and understanding. But don't let this put you off joining: they are friendly, helpful and more than willing to welcome you into their world. Before you begin to show you need to join the BRC in order to get the identity rings that must be worn by all show rabbits.

If you start exhibiting, you will no doubt catch the bug to start breeding your animals. Of course you don't have to show to breed, you may merely want to breed youngsters to pass on to your friends or even to add to the household's diet. There are many books available, from the British Rabbit Council and your local library, about keeping rabbits as pets and about showing and breeding.

It is usual to put the doe into the buck's cage for mating, that is, into the more dominant animal's territory. If she is not ready for mating she will soon make this quite clear and should be removed forthwith. If she is ready, she will lie flat on the floor with her hindquarters raised and mating will soon occur. There is no sure way of knowing if a mating has been successful, though one clue is that a male who has ejaculated usually makes a squeaking noise and falls sideways off the female. Many breeders reintroduce the doe to the buck a couple of days after the first mating to ensure successful fertilization.

As with wild rabbits, pregnancy in the domestic breeds lasts about thirty days. A few days before giving birth the mother-to-be should be given a nest box and some form of bedding material such as hay from which she can make a nest which she will line with fur pulled from her belly and flanks. Make sure she is kept quiet with a plentiful supply of food and water and all is likely to go well.

Finally, do not be in too much of a hurry to look at the babies: a lot of disturbance early on may cause the mother to desert or destroy her babies. Providing you see movement in the nest, the doe seems content, her nipples have enlarged and look suckled then all is probably OK and it is best to leave well alone until the young emerge of their own accord some twelve days after birth.

If you do think something is amiss, then gently remove the mother from the cage and carefully look in the nest – touching the young as little as possible. You may find some dead youngsters or some that have been cannibalized. If the doe has not been suckled within 48 hours of the birth and the young look weak, then you may want to try and hand rear them. You may succeed by keeping the young warm and feeding a few cc. of a made-up milk powder daily. But don't be too down-hearted if death ensues as baby rabbits are difficult to hand rear.

Rabbits can be a great source of pleasure, simply as loved family pets or, for the more interested, as a fascinating hobby. Personally, I have never shown rabbits but I have bred plenty both as a child and an adult. Of course, I have my favourites, most notably an intrepid white rabbit of unknown lineage (certainly not pure bred) aptly called Nomad, who was a great escape artist and severely tested the ingenuity of my mother's cage-building skills throughout the eleven years of his life. I have always found rabbits interesting and rewarding animals to keep.

Fancy that!

Rabbits have been kept in people's back yards on a large scale since the Enclosure of Land Acts of the 18th century. These acts meant that cottagers could no longer graze their cows or sheep on common land. A realistic alternative was to keep a few rabbits in the yard for the cooking pot. The exhibiting of fancy rabbits grew out of the Industrial Revolution when country folk went to work in factories and mills. Living in small terraced houses with no more than a small back yard, they were unable to indulge their country tradition of keeping much in the way of livestock. But there was space to keep a few rabbits and pigeons and, if neighbours too kept such beasts, then quite soon friendly competitions for who bred the prettiest or longest-eared rabbit would occur, as indeed did competitions for pigeon racing. These competitions soon resulted in clubs being formed and now there are hundreds of local rabbit fancier clubs throughout the country. The emergence of better and faster forms of transport meant that distant clubs could compete against one another, resulting in the many championship shows held today.

Out of all this, many fancy breeds have been developed, each with its own history. The Angora is one of the earliest English breeds (originally called the Angolan) and is the only breed kept for its wool. Just like the sheep, the rabbit is clipped for its silky fleece which, when spun, can be knitted up into fine (and expensive) garments. Another rabbit bred for its coat texture, rather than colour, is the Rex. First bred in 1919 in France and Germany, these rabbits have a mutant gene which results in a very short dense coat with short guard hairs, giving it a velvety feel. Of course, a major factor to be bred for in fancy rabbits is colour and markings. The Chinchilla rabbit was originally developed by careful breeding for the fur trade in the 1920s. The objective was to develop a fur that resembled the real chinchilla as much as possible and thus provide a cheap substitute for those who could not afford a coat made of the real thing. Perhaps the oddest fancy rabbit standards apply to the English. Breeders have tried, so far unsuccessfully, to produce a rabbit with identical markings to those described in 1849. These markings include a butterfly-shaped smut on the nose, large circles around the eyes and a spot on each cheek, rather like a fashionable Regency lady. The ears too are coloured and there is a herringbone pattern running along the spine. Along each side there should be a chain of spots which widens to decorate the loins. Each leg should be

The English Rabbit.

adorned with a single spot and the belly with six. The tail should be pure white. The English is probably the only animal whose ideal was known even before people started to breed it in earnest.

As well as the recognized fancy breed standards, there have been rabbits bred to outdo records. For instance, the longest ears on a rabbit measured over 70cm (27.5 inches) – the poor animal wasn't able to move them. A Frenchman developed a breed with an incredibly long back, known as Accordian Giants. However, the record for domestic rabbits must be awarded to one of the Angevin breed, now extinct, which reputedly weighed 15kg (33lb) and was over 1·5m (5 feet) long. The present-day record is held by a female of the French Lop breed who, when exhibited in Spain in 1980 at the tender age of 5 months, weighed 12·01kg (26·67lb), more than twice the average weight for her breed. The largest breed of rabbit is the aptly named Flemish Giant. These measure up to 0·91m (3 feet) when fully stretched and weights up to 11·3kg (25lb) have been reliably recorded. This is pretty big when compared to the average size of a wild rabbit, a mere 1·58kg (3·5lb). The big daddy of the wild bunnies was one shot in 1982 in Scotland who weighed 3·74kg (8lb 4oz), the size of a newborn human.

Another rabbity record belongs to a New Zealand White doe who in 1978 gave birth to and reared 24 young in a single litter. Finally, the grande dame of the bunny world. This title must surely go to Flopsy, a pet rabbit who lived in Tasmania and who died in 1983 at the ripe old age of 18 years 10·5 months. So again make sure you really want a pet rabbit, yours may even beat Flopsy's record.

Lust and luck

In common with many animals, rabbits and hares have become the unwitting target of human thoughts and imaginings. This process has been going on throughout the evolution of modern man. The earliest evidence we have of this cultural connection with the *Lagomorpha* is in palaeolithic art of around 25,000 BC. An image of a hare with its characteristically prominent eye is scored into the rock wall of a cave at Le Gabillou in the Dordogne region of France. Another fine example of this early art is on a fragment of stone found near the French resort of Biarritz. We can never know the significance of these images to the people who made them. It seems reasonable to suppose that they may have had a religious or magical purpose, perhaps connected with hunting (or perhaps people just liked drawing).

Since those remote times, men (and women) have observed, worshipped, hunted and protected rabbits and hares in a bewildering diversity of ways. Rabbits and hares are distinct species with markedly different habits. However, throughout history there often has been a complete confusion between them and even between them and totally different

species. One very early work where this happened was the Old Testament of the Bible. In *Leviticus*, Moses tells his people which foods they cannot eat, one of which was 'the coney, because he cheweth the cud, but divideth not the hoof.' (*Leviticus*, 11, 5). The trouble is, there were no coneys (that is, rabbits) in Palestine at the time of Moses. It is more likely that he was referring to the rock badger or hyrax, a rodent indigenous to the region. However, the translators of the King James version of the Bible either chose to overlook, or couldn't handle, this level of zoological refinement and opted for a more familiar equivalent. So generations of rabbits can be grateful for this confusion which led them to feature on the unclean list rather than the menu. Needless to say, this didn't actually prevent them from being hunted and eaten.

In the next verse to the one quoted above, Moses consigns hares to the unclean group using exactly the same words. Strictly speaking, neither rabbits nor hares (nor hyraxes) chew the cud, though the digestion process of the hares and rabbits serves a similar function. In this respect the translators got it right as hares certainly lived in that part of the world at the time of Moses.

While the Bible brought confusion between rabbits and hyraxes, the slave trade brought confusion between rabbits and hares. In Africa the hare was a common animal and it featured strongly in stories and mythology. There, the hare played the same role as Reynard the Fox played in European culture; a shrewd and quick-witted character. When Africans were enslaved and shipped to America they naturally took their traditions with them. In America there were no hares or rabbits as the Africans and Europeans knew them. There were the somewhat similar-looking and related species of North American cottontails. When they first set eyes on these animals, the English settlers said, 'Ah, rabbits,' and the slaves said, 'Ah, hares,' in much the same way as the Phoenicians earlier had said, 'Ah, rock hyraxes,' when they first saw rabbits in Spain.

The upshot of all this was that the wily African hare resurfaced as the wily Brer Rabbit in the famous Uncle Remus tales. In the illustrations, Brer Rabbit looks remarkably, though not surprisingly, like an American cottontail. A more recent American cultural figure is Bugs Bunny who, despite his name, resembles a cottontail more than a bunny. It is not really surprising that in the popular mind hares, rabbits and cottontails are all inextricably entangled.

Alongside and in contrast to this history of mistakes and confusion runs a tradition of practical knowledge and patient observation. In 1387, Gaston II, then Count of Foix in France, wrote a detailed book on hunting. Amongst other useful tips he writes that, 'Men know by the outer side of the hare's leg if she is passed a year.' He was probably referring to the head of the large shin bone, the tibia. In young rabbits and hares this has a distinct notch which can be felt with a thumbnail.

Gaston's text has survived in many manuscripts. In a fifteenth-century version the illustrator clearly and correctly portrays a hare nursing her young in an upright position. However, it is a measure of the mixture of knowledge and confusion that, in the same manuscript, the illustrations of rabbits are indistinguishable from those of hares, the only clues being given in the text or, as in the above example, by what the animal is doing. And yet the fifteenth century, during which this illustrator worked, saw an increase in realistic art. This is exemplified by the beautiful watercolour of a hare done by Albrecht Durer at the end of this period in 1502.

'Lockpicking' – detail from Greene (1591), illustrating the 'thief-like' qualities attributed to rabbits.

Returning to Gaston's time in the late 1300s: then, as now, while people like Gaston studied animals for their own sake (albeit sparked off by his interest in hunting), there was an alternative and concurrent use of animals in culture. This was the widespread employment of animals as symbols; rabbits and hares (and generally an indeterminate mixture of the two) were used in a great range of roles.

The rabbit often represented carnal love, that is lust, and was frequently portrayed as an associate of Venus, the goddess of love. In the 1470s an Italian court painter, Francesco del Cossa, painted an exotic mural on the walls of the Palazzo Schifanoia in Ferrara. The mural depicts symbols of the months of the year, including astrological signs, mythical gods and scenes of country and courtly life. One scene is of the Garden of Love.

Detail from Cosimo's painting of Venus.

Venus is on an elaborate chariot around which young people disport themselves in a variety of amorous poses and a positive plague of rabbits carpets the ground. In the same tradition, another Italian Renaissance artist, Piero di Cosimo, depicts in a painting Venus, Mars and several cupids. Peering over Venus's naked body is one of the cupids and a very large rabbit (or hare?) with handsome black-tipped ears.

Around the time of Durer the animals still kept their symbolic role, but often were more carefully drawn. Another Italian, Pisanello, drew Luxuria and a rabbit. Luxuria is the female personification of the original sin of sexual temptation and excess while the rabbit symbolizes lust. In Titian's 'Madonna and the Rabbit', painted about 1530, the symbolic meaning of the Madonna's hand on a white rabbit is of the pure Virgin Mary holding lust in check. All these pictures are kept abroad, but an early picture of a hare is in the National Gallery in London. It is by Pisanello and called 'The Vision of St Eustace'. Amongst a variety of animals in the picture there is, in the bottom right-hand corner, a hare being pursued by a hound.

The association of the rabbit with sin and lust is an example of how animals can become the symbols of something morally bad. A similar process seems to have affected the hare. In common with other creatures, it had been a sacred and symbolic creature in the old, pre-Christian religions of Europe. It was an omen which could be used for fortune telling. It is said that, before going into battle, Boadicea, Queen of the Ancient Britons, would release a hare which she had previously hidden in her bosom. The animals would run off and, on the basis of its twists and turns, the outcome of the ensuing battle could be predicted.

With the coming of Christianity, the symbols of the old religion lost their sacred and morally neutral character. Instead they became fixed as symbols of bad luck. It was unlucky for a hare to cross the path in front of you. In the North, if a fisherman on the way to his boat met a hare he would turn back – he would have no luck that day. For a pregnant woman seeing a hare was worse, meaning that either she would miscarry or that the child would be born with a hare-lip. The hare was also an omen of death.

This fearful aspect of the hare was linked with the belief that it was a familiar of witches. A witch could freely transform herself into the shape of a hare, and therefore any hare one saw was likely to be a witch in disguise. Amongst other feats, the hare-witch could suck a cow dry and could only be killed by a silver cross or, in more recent versions, shot with a silver bullet. These beliefs were very powerful and the lives of many were haunted by superstitious fear of people such as Isabel Gowdie. Isabel was a Scottish witch who lived in the 1700s and who left a record of her incantations. The spell to change herself into a hare was:

> I sall goe intill ane haire
> With sorrow, and sych, and meikle caire,
> And I sall go in the Divellis nam,
> Ay whill I com hom againe.

The incantation to perform the change in the reverse direction was:

> Hare, hare, God send thee care.
> I am in an hare's likeness just now,
> But I shall be in a woman's likeness even now.

It has been a longstanding tradition to consider the hare as evil, fearful and a bringer of bad luck. There is a late thirteenth-century poem composed almost entirely of some 70, mostly slanderous, names for the hare. According to the poem the hare's strength (as a bringer of bad luck) can only be overcome by the recitation of the list. We can get a feel of the dread with which people viewed the hare by some of the epithets they used to describe it. The hare is called 'make-agrise', the thing that makes people shudder; 'make-fare', the one that makes people flee; and 'the der that no-mon ne-der nemnen', the animal so taboo that no one dare name it.

Of course, men's supersititious dread did not prevent the hare from systematically being hunted and trapped from the earliest times. But just

118

as there have always been hunters and celebrations of hunting, so too there have been people who have gone against this trend.

One early defender was St Monacella or Melengell who became the patron saint of hares. In 604 AD Brochwel Ysgythrog, the Prince and Earl of Chester, was out hunting one day. He and his dogs pursued a hare into a large thicket of bramble. Upon penetrating the brambles the prince found a beautiful maiden kneeling quite still and praying devoutly. The hare was lying under the edge of her dress. In this position it seemed to have lost all its fear and boldly stared at the prince and his hounds. The prince urged his dogs on to kill the hare but, the more he urged, the more they cowered, whimpered and retreated. Finally the prince gave up and, in recognition of her piety, gave the land to Melengell as a sanctuary for the rest of her life. It is said that for the remaining 37 years of her life wild hares gathered around her like tame animals.

The English saint, St Godric, also became a protector of hares. He would release hares caught in snares and if one was fleeing from huntsmen he would take it into his house and protect it until the hunt had gone.

It is not only saints who have shown compassion for hares. Thomas Bewick, the famous nineteenth-century natural history illustrator, writes that his feelings for animals were first aroused when he was a boy. He caught a hare while it was surrounded by hunters and dogs. The terrified animal was screaming like a child in a most heart-rending manner and the boy's thoughts were solely on how to save its life. Many authorities have pointed out the extraordinary similarity between the scream of a hare, or rabbit, and that of a child. This kind of resemblance seems to be a powerful force underlying our traditional identifications with some animals and not others.

In George Ewart Evans's book, *The Leaping Hare*, an East Anglian farmer felt moved to comment that he believed that beagling was more cruel than hare coursing. He recited an incident of his own experience which had helped confirm this belief. On one occasion he shot a hare while it was on the run from the hounds. 'I shot it and covered it up so the hounds didn't find it. Well, when I opened that hare I was never so surprised. There wasn't a mite of blood in it! That blood was all gone to pink bubbles. She'd been chased then for over a quarter of an hour and her blood was all gone to pink bubbles.' The complete lack of blood and presence of pink bubbles is most certainly a striking image and we naturally seek an explanation for this phenomenon. Unfortunately, this evocative description does not give enough information to allow any convincing physiological explanation to be made.

Even in this brief look at historical rabbits and hares, the diversity and potency of feelings and beliefs connected with these animals is quite striking. Rabbits and hares have been in favour and out of favour, but they've rarely been just boring or irrelevant.

Samuel Pepys improves his luck

We have all heard of the superstition that keeping a rabbit's foot in your pocket wards off bad luck and ill health, particularly arthritis. The origins of this folk belief are lost to time, but it seems that the hare's foot was once considered an equally potent charm. Samuel Pepys, the famous British diarist, and his friend Mr Batten shared the fashionable belief that a hare's foot would protect them from colic, an illness which we know as stomach ache. For as Pepys notes in his diary:

Dec 31st, 1664: So ends the old yeare, I bless God, with great joy to me, and not only from my having made so good a year of profit . . . but I bless God I have never been in so good plight as to my health in so very cold weather as this, nor indeed in any hot weather, these ten years as I am this day. . . . But I am at a great losse to know whether it be my hare's foote, or taking every morning a pill of turpentine, or my having left off the wearing of a gown.

Unfortunately for Pepys, this period of good health was interrupted in the middle of January. But, thanks to good

'medical' advice there was a happy end to the story. His diary continues:

Jan 19th, 1665: Memorandum. This day and yesterday, I think it is the change of the weather, I have a great deal of pain, but nothing like I used to have. I can hardly keep myself loose, but on the contrary am forced to drive away my pain.

Jan 20th, 1665: So homeward, in my way buying a hare and taking it home, which upon my discourse with Mr Batten in Westminster Hall, who showed me my mistake that my hare's foote hath not the joynte in it; and assures me he never had his cholique since he carried it about him: and it is a strange thing how fancy works, for I no sooner almost handled his foote but my belly began to be loose and to break wind, and whereas I was in some pain yesterday and tother day and in fear of more today, I became very well and so continue.

So, clearly, one must be exact with one's good luck charms: a foot without the joint is ineffectual. It's interesting that the somewhat down-to-earth Pepys should place such trust in his hare's foot, especially as, in referring to his fancy, he seems to be aware that the potency of his charm is at least partly psychological.

Rabbits for children, bunnies for grown-ups

In our own modern times, rabbits and hares have continued to pop up in our culture. Interestingly, whereas in the past the strongest and richest associations seem to have been with the hare, in the twentieth century it is the rabbit that has become predominant. It seems likely that this reflects the growth in population of the rabbit and the decline in that of the hare, and the fact that the rabbit is a common domestic pet.

One pet rabbit has certainly achieved immortality. Peter Rabbit was the product of the creative imagination of Beatrix Potter. He was based on her real-life pet of the same name. From infancy, Beatrix had been immensely attached to animals and nature in general. Although born in London, she had spent a lot of her childhood in the country on the regular holidays taken with her parents. On her first trip to a farm she immediately found herself at home with the collies, cows and pigs. In fact, she seemed more at ease with the animals than she did with grown-up people. Nor was this strong connection sentimental or squeamish. She and her younger brother found and smuggled home all kinds of things: beetles, toadstools, dead birds, hedgehogs. On one occasion they even brought home a dead fox. The two budding zoologists skinned it, boiled the carcase to remove the flesh and articulated the skeleton.

It is not surprising then that Beatrix Potter's charming stories contain a realistic acceptance of the violence and danger which are part and parcel of an animal's life. Peter Rabbit's father had an accident: 'he was put in a pie by Mrs McGregor.' When Peter himself is pursued, Mr McGregor brandishes a rake, nearly succeeds in trapping Peter under a garden sieve and in squashing him under his boot; Peter ends up 'trembling with fright'.

Together with the direct, un-slushy narrative, Beatrix Potter also drew the illustrations. She was a talented artist and this, combined with a close observation of the animal's physique and behaviour, resulted in pictures where the animals are humanized in that they wear clothes and walk upright but in which they still retain the essential characteristics of their species. So her rabbits look like rabbits, do rabbity things and get chased and sometimes caught like real rabbits.

Peter Rabbit was first published in 1901. It and Beatrix Potter's subsequent books have become perennial favourites. They are considered classic English children's books. This is not only a tribute to the author but also another example of the ancient and continuing connection between animals and man and how animals stimulate our imagination.

Though *Peter Rabbit* is still widely read, he perhaps is not a character to which many of today's children can easily relate. Peter dates from a time when Britain was more rural, he is not part of our post-war urban culture. He is neither a city slicker nor Hollywood star. Films and television have kept the tradition of the fictional rabbit alive as much as have books. In Walt Disney's film 'Bambi', the young fawn's companion is a cuddly, friendly rabbit called Thumper, a character of the same ilk as Peter. Not so Bugs Bunny. Bugs is perhaps the ultimate modern rabbit. He is a sophisticated, wise-cracking creature who is streetwise and hip. In contrast, Richard Adams's book, and subsequent film, *Watership Down*, seem more in the tradition of Beatrix Potter in so far as it remains closer to the actual world of rabbits. This is not surprising since the book is based on R.M. Lockley's popular scientific work, *The Private Life of the Rabbit*. However, we can see Adams discarding the clear unsentimentality of the Potter tradition and overlaying a more human and emotional plot.

In the adult world, one peculiarly modern use of the rabbit image is the Bunny Girl. In fact, she was a two-stage invention. In 1953, Hugh Hefner was struggling to get the first edition of *Playboy* magazine together. He needed a logo, one which he felt would embody the personality of the magazine. Inspiration struck: a rabbit in a tuxedo. Why a rabbit? Well, because he felt this portrayed the qualities of cuteness, sexiness and friskiness. It seems that Hefner had, perhaps unwittingly, made the connection of the rabbit with carnal sin. It is indicative of the so-called permissive age that an image which used to carry a significant charge of moral disapproval was now merely seen as cute.

By 1959, *Playboy* magazine was a great success and Hefner was looking for ways to expand his business. Clubs seemed to be the answer, and a key feature of the clubs was to be attractive waitresses, called 'playmates'. There was considerable discussion about what these waitresses would wear. Ilsa Taurius, a friend, suggested that their costume should be based on the original rabbit logo. Hefner had apparently briefly considered this option but had rejected it because the logo was definitely male. But Ilsa was persuasive and her mother was a seamstress who could and did put together a prototype female rabbit outfit at short notice.

So we must credit Ilsa for the idea and her mother for the first version of the bunny costume. Within days Ilsa was modelling the satin corset which

had a fluffy ball attached to the backside. On her head she wore a pair of rabbity ears. At first some people had doubts, but Hefner was pleased, he liked the tail. A few modifications, raising the corset above the thigh, adding a collar, nifty bow tie and cuffs, and the Bunny Girl was born.

This history is curious, not just because the rabbit changed sex. More interesting is the transformation from the humanized rabbit to the rabbitized human. The original logo was of a rabbit made sophisticated and human by its tuxedo dress. In the Bunny Girl, we have a human made sexy, cute and frisky by the addition of a fluffy tail and floppy ears.

One extremely venerable rabbit who is still alive and kicking today is the Easter Bunny. The roots of this tradition go back to the pre-Christian period. Spring festivals were universal and have existed since the earliest times. In northern Europe this festival was held in honour of Eastre, the Teutonic goddess of dawn. The hare was believed to be her favourite animal and attendant spirit. It was thought that Eastre brought lights and that the hares actually carried them. (As an aside, it is interesting that in Chinese tradition the hare is associated with the fourth two-hour period of the day, that is, sunrise). Eastre also represented spring fecundity and, by extension, the love and carnal pleasure which lead to fecundity. Here we can see a source for another of the frequently quoted attributes of rabbits and hares.

When the new Christian festival arrived, it did not replace the old festival of Eastre but was grafted onto the existing one. One consequence of this is that we call our Christian festival by its ancient, pagan name of Easter. Another consequence is the continuing presence of Easter rabbits (originally hares) and Easter eggs. Eggs symbolize the spring forces of creation and re-creation. There is a traditional English Easter game of searching for Easter eggs thought to have been laid by the Easter Bunny. At first glance the notion of an egg-laying rabbit seems absurd. It is only when we uncover the deeper, symbolic meaning of eggs, hares and the spring festival that it begins to make some sense.

The Easter Bunny makes a fitting tail-piece (sorry!) to our brief survey of rabbits and hares in folklore and culture. He unites the most ancient times with the present in one unbroken tradition.

We have only touched upon the complex and contradictory traditions surrounding hares and rabbits which have grown up in this country and Europe. Equally rich traditions exist in the cultures of the East, Africa and America. These have received but the barest of mentions. And yet the predominant note for us today is none of these, valuable and interesting though they are. For us, the overriding issue is the recognition and valuation of animals in their own right, unencumbered by our human wishes and fears. As the human power to destroy and pollute the natural world has grown, so has a widespread sensitivity and sense of responsibility towards the natural world. In order that we can better understand its components and inter-relationships, we need knowledge. The way of life and habits of the *Lagomorpha* is just one small facet of this wider quest. But even in this small area there are big gaps in our understanding, particularly of their behaviour in the wild. There is still plenty of room for that sense of wonder at these, still mysterious, creatures.

The year of the rabbit

For billions of people 1987, or rather January 29th, 1987 to February 16th, 1988, was not just another year. It was the Year of the Rabbit, and Chinese communities all over the world celebrated appropriately with colourful processions and fireworks.

In Chinese culture the years go by in cycles of twelve, each year being associated with an animal, one of which is the rabbit – or is it the hare? There is a degree of confusion between the two arising from the translation from the Chinese to English. The Chinese have a single word for both animals interpreted as either rabbit or hare. Well, it keeps up the longstanding tradition of confusion between the two species.

As in Western astrology, each Chinese year is divided into twelve signs of the zodiac. These are also associated with an animal. In order, the Chinese zodiac signs are; rat, ox, tiger, hare, dragon, snake, horse, sheep, monkey, cock, dog and pig. If your sign is the hare, which roughly corresponds to our March, then you are a sociable person, though somewhat aloof. You are likely to be artistic, kind and try to avoid confrontations, but you are rather a gossip. It is advised that as far as relationships go, you should avoid people born under the sign of the rat, dragon or cock. Better stick to those who share your own sign or were born under the ox, dog or pig. Specially favoured relationships are indicated between hare-people, sheep-people and snake-people.

For hare-people, according to the Chinese belief, the Year of the Rabbit is fortunate. The next such year is 1999–2000 AD, so hare-people will have the privilege of spanning the millennia: even more special.

Finally, two more pearls of oriental wisdom. Whereas we say the 'man in the moon', the Chinese refer to the 'hare in the moon'. In their mythology the hare that lives in the moon pounds the herbs making the elixir of life. They have a saying, 'When the hare dies, the fox mourns.' This is the equivalent of our saying, 'There but for the grace of God go I'.

Further information

Cowan, D., *The Wild Rabbit* (Blandford Press, London, 1980)
Evans, G.E., and D. Thomson, *The Leaping Hare* (Faber and Faber, London, 1972)
Lockley, R.M., *The Private Life of the Rabbit* (Deutsch, London, 1964)
Sandford, J.C., *The Domestic Rabbit* (Crosby, Lockwood, 1957)
Scott, G.R., *Rabbit Keeping* (David & Charles, Newton Abbot, 1979)
Sheail, J., *Rabbits and Their History* (David & Charles, Newton Abbot, 1971)
Tapper, S., *The Brown Hare* (Shire, Princes Risborough, 1987)
Tittensor, A.M. and H.G. Lloyd, *Rabbits* (HMSO, London, 1983)

British Rabbit Council, Purefoy House, 7 Kirkgate, Nottinghamshire NG24 1AD
Fur and Feather, 37–9 Fyled Rd, Preston, Lancashire PR1 2KQ
Game Conservancy Council, Burgate Manor, Fordingbridge, Hampshire
MAFF, Tangley Place, Worplesdon, Surrey GU3 3JZ
Mammal Society, c/o Linnean Society, Burlington House, Piccadilly, London W1V 0LQ

Index